DASH DIET

COOKBOOK

For Beginners

2022

---

365 Days of Quick & Easy Low Sodium Recipes to Lower Your Blood Pessure | 30-Day Meal Plan Full of Healthy Foods to Improve Your Hearth Wellness

---

Sheila J. Baker

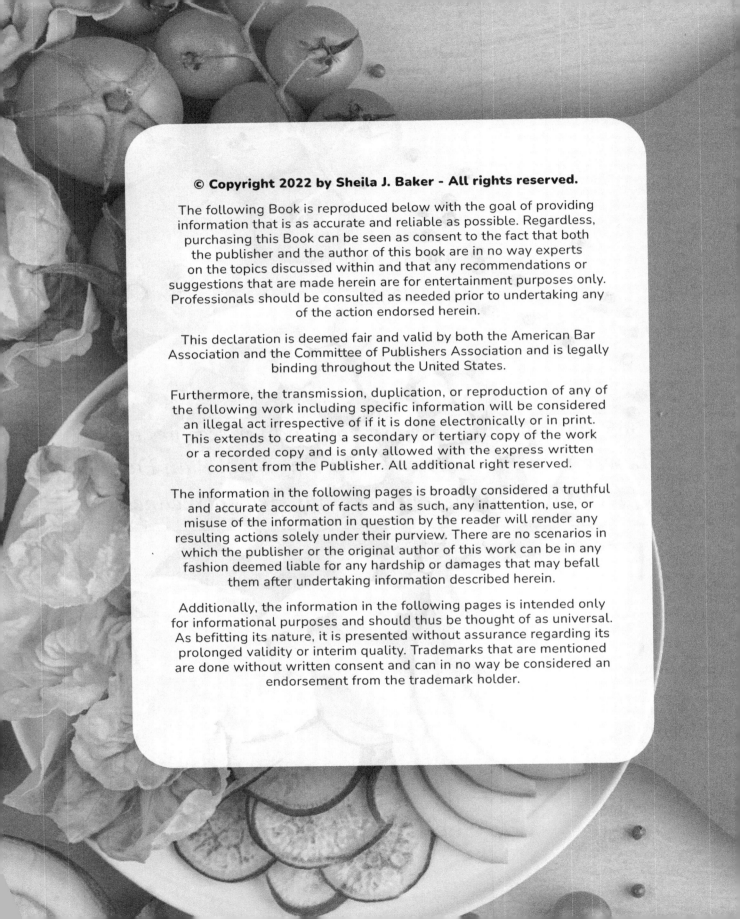

CONTENTS

INTRODUCTION

Generally speaking, most people who are looking to start the DASH diet are people who suffer from high blood pressure themselves or have a family member that does.

Men are more likely to have hypertension issues, especially after the age of 45, and a significant amount of patients with diabetes will experience these symptoms as well. Also, put at risk are individuals who are overweight. However, hypertension can happen to anyone.

DASH is an acronym for Dietary Approaches to Stop Hypertension. The diet is centered on eating a balanced combination of lean meats, vegetables, whole grains, and fruits, and keeping sodium intake between two-thirds and one tablespoon of salt per day depending on the reasons for starting the diet and the results you are seeking.

The DASH diet also focuses on keeping fats, added sugars, and red meat to a lower level. As with all diets, there is a happy medium for keeping true to the diet.

When you experience the symptoms of hypertension for extended amounts of time, you are more at risk for heart disease, kidney issues, and higher glucose levels leading to diabetes. You also are at a higher risk of early mortality.

However, following the simple to understand guidelines of the DASH Diet will help to bring your blood pressure numbers to a more manageable level and help you to be healthier in the long run, bringing your chances of living a much more fulfilling life for you.

When you work towards your goals on the DASH Diet, you will start to see the results rather quickly which will help you to keep your willpower working towards your personal goals.

The DASH diet is a fantastic approach to stay healthy, lose weight, and enhance your general well-being. And it can be used by vegetarians too.

But again, remember that this is just one way of eating. You must be making healthy food choices for yourself. And sticking to the rules of the DASH diet is just one way to do that. You may want to include some other diet or eating plan into your lifestyle as well. For instance, you could use Dash Diet as part of a balanced plan for weight loss and good health.

UNDERSTANDING THE DASH DIET

Dietary Approaches to Stop Hypertension is one of the most effective organic treatments of all health problems related to high blood pressure or fluid build-up in the body. These approaches come with a complete program, which places emphasis on the diet as well as lifestyle changes. Commonly called the DASH diet, the major target is to reduce the sodium content of your diet by omitting table salt directly or reducing the intake through other ingredients. There are two minerals that work against each other to maintain the body fluid balance: those are sodium and potassium. In perfect proportions, these two control the release and retention of fluids in the body. In the case of environmental or genetic complexities or a high sodium diet, the balance is disturbed so much that it puts our heart at risk by elevating systolic and diastolic blood pressures.

Origin of the DASH Diet

This dietary plan came to the knowledge of nutritionists after several research studies were conducted to treat hypertension focused on diet in order to avoid medication's side effects. It was seen as a way to reduce the blood pressure using healthy, nourishing food and following an active routine. The main goal was to cure hypertension, so it was soon termed as the Dietary Approaches to Stop Hypertension (DASH). However, its broad-scale effects showed greater efficiency than just reducing hypertension, and people started using it to treat obesity, diabetes, cancer, and cardiac disorders.

To study the impact of sodium intake, a scientist used three experimental groups. Each group was assigned a diet with varying sodium levels. One was to take 3300 mg sodium per day; the second had to use 2300 mg per day, and the third one was put on a diet having 1500 mg sodium per day, about two-thirds of a teaspoon of salt. By restricting the sodium content, all participants showed decreased blood pressure. But the group with the least amount of sodium intake showed the most alleviation in the blood pressure levels. Thus, it was identified that 1500 mg of sodium per day is the threshold amount to maintain blood pressure.

Health Advantages of the DASH Diet

Besides hypertension, there are several health advantages that later came to light as experts recorded the conditions people experience after choosing the diet. Here are some of the most acknowledged benefits of the DASH diet:

Alleviated Blood Pressure

It is the most obvious and direct outcome of this dietary routine as it restricts the sodium intake, which rightly reduces the risks of high blood pressure by keeping the blood consistency to near normal. People with hypertension disorder should restrict sodium intake the most, whereas others should keep the intake as per the described limits, 1500 mg per day.

Maintained Cholesterol Levels

Since a DASH diet promotes greater use of vegetables, fruits, whole grains, beans, and nuts, it can provide enough fiber to regulate our metabolism and digestive functions. Moreover, it promotes only lean meats and no saturated fats, which also helps to maintain cholesterol levels in the body. Such fats have to be replaced with healthy cholesterol fats to keep the heart running.

Weight Maintenance

Weight loss is another primary objective for people on the DASH diet. With a nutritious and clean diet, anyone can lose their excess weight. Moreover, the DASH diet also promotes proper physical exercise every day, which also proves to be significant in reducing obesity. Sometimes, obesity is the result of inflammation or fluid imbalances in the body, and the DASH diet can even cure that through its progressive health approach.

Reduced Risks of Osteoporosis

Osteoporosis is the degeneration of the bones, and there are many factors associated with it; at the base of it is the decrease of calcium and vitamin D in the body. The DASH diet provides ways and meals to fill this deficiency gap and reduce the risks of osteoporosis, especially in women.

Healthier Kidneys

Kidneys are what control the fluid balance of the body with the help of hormones and minerals. So, a smart diet that is designed with the sole purpose of aiding kidney functions can keep them healthy and functioning properly. Excess salt or oxalate intake can cause kidney stones. The DASH diet reduces the chances of these stones from building up in the kidneys.

Protection From Cancer

The DASH diet has been proven successful in preventing people from different types of cancer, like kidney, lung, prostate, esophagus, rectum, and colon cancers. The diet co-joins all the important factors which can fight against cancer and help prevent the development of cancerous cells.

Prevention From Diabetes

The DASH diet is effective in reducing insulin resistance, which is one of the common causes of diabetes in many people. Reduced weight, an active metabolism, maintained body fluids, daily exercises, increased water consumption, a low sodium diet, and a healthy gut or digestive system are all the factors that link the DASH diet with the reduced risks of diabetes in a person.

Improved Mental Health

Mental health is largely dependent on the type of food you eat. Anxiety, depression, and insomnia are all the outcomes of poor health and a bad lifestyle. The entire neural transmission is controlled by the electrolyte balance in the nervous system. With the DASH diet, you can create optimum conditions for efficient brain functions.

Less Risk of Heart Disease

Since the DASH diet is designed to control the varying blood pressure, it saves the heart from the negative impact of high blood pressure and prevents it from different diseases. Constant high blood pressure burdens the heart and causes the weakening of its walls and valves. Such risks are reduced with the help of the DASH diet.

The DASH Dietary Program

It's not just the sodium on which the DASH diet focuses; there are various forms and types of food that it limits. It also places a large emphasis on a certain amount of food per serving. It creates a special place or a box of food for the entire day and limits your daily intake to a value that would maintain a balance in the diet. Such control is hard to attain when you are not following the DASH diet, as the diet prescribes the entire roadmap to better dietary solutions. It is designed to change the ways we see our food and the way we consume it. It mainly works in two ways. First, it controls the quality of the meal, and second, it controls the quantity of the meal. By doing this, you can achieve increased health benefits that no other diet could guarantee. The food is first placed into categories, like fruits, vegetables, whole grains, beans, nuts, meat, or dairy, then you consider the health impact of each category; their share in a single meal or serving is suggested.

Research-Based Benefits of DASH Dieting

The National Institute of Health in the United States carried out early research on the significance of the DASH Diet. Scientists knew the impact of such a diet, but they needed proof to strengthen their claim. So, three different dietary plans were designed to check the impact. The plan with the most fruits, vegetables, beans, and no fat dairy items came out as the most effective in decreasing the diastolic and systolic blood pressures by 3 mmHg and 6 mmHg, respectively. While the DASH diet sets a limitation on certain food items, it also directs a person to controlled caloric intake. It keeps the daily caloric intake between 1600 to 3100. This fact becomes more important when there is obesity that has to be dealt with. By passing the Optimal Macronutrient Intake Trial for heart health, the DASH diet set the record of successfully reducing the routine fat intake, preventing all sorts of heart diseases.

It's a Long-Term Solution

Hypertension sufferers cannot always count on medications for long term health stability. No matter how effective the medicines are, they are not free from side effects. A change in diet and lifestyle can give long term treatment along with necessary prevention. Hypertension is not a temporary disorder; once a person has it, they are forever bound by this problem. It is not a matter of days, it's a matter of the rest of their life. That is why only dietary treatment can save the body from high blood pressure and the problems associated with it.

Helps Manage Type 2 Diabetes

To understand the relevance between the DASH diet and diabetes, it is important to look into the root causes of Type 2 Diabetes. High caloric food or increased body weight both make the body resistant to insulin. When you cross off both those factors, it becomes easier to control Type 2 Diabetes. The DASH diet works to manage both these factors. Firstly, through its regulated serving technique and secondly, through reducing obesity. It increases insulin sensitivity in the body.; thus, it decreases the possible risks of high blood sugar levels. Moreover, with the dietary balance the DASH diet creates, it sets the bar for carbohydrate consumption, and in the absence of excess carbohydrates, the body can regulate its insulin production and its functions.

Ten Reasons Why the DASH Diet Truly Works

When we talk about the DASH diet outside of theory and more in actuality, we can see how effective it is as a diet. Aside from extensive research and experimentation, the underlying reasons for people's interest in this diet are its specific characteristics. It provides a sense of ease and convenience, allowing consumers to feel more at ease with its laws and regulations.Here are some of the reasons why the DASH Diet works amazingly:

Easy to Adopt

The wide range of foods offered under the DASH diet label makes it more adaptable for everyone. This is why many find it easier to make the switch and reap the genuine health benefits. It allows consumers to be more adaptable.

Promotes Exercise

It is the most successful of all the variables since it not only emphasizes regular exercises and routine physical activities, but it also emphasizes food and its consumption. This is why it provides immediate and apparent results.

All Inclusive

With few restrictions, this diet has incorporated every food item with minor adjustments. It correctly instructs us on the Dos and Don'ts of all ingredients, preventing us from ingesting those that are damaging to our bodies and health.

A Well Balanced Approach

One of its most significant benefits is that it helps us maintain balance in our diet, routine, caloric intake, and nutrition.

Good Caloric Check

On the DASH diet, every meal is pre-calculated in terms of calories. We can simply keep track of our daily caloric intake and, as a result, reduce it by eliminating particular foods.

Prohibits Bad Food

The DASH diet encourages the consumption of more organic and fresh foods while discouraging the consumption of processed foods and store-bought junk food. As a result, the users' eating habits improve.

Focused on Prevention

It is described as more of a preventive strategy than a cure for many diseases, despite the fact that it has been demonstrated to be a cure for numerous ailments.

Slow Yet Progressive Changes

The diet isn't overly restrictive, and it allows for progressive alterations as you work toward your ultimate health objective. You can set daily, weekly, or even monthly goals whenever it is convenient for you.

Long Term Effects

The DASH diet not only produces amazing results, but it also has a long-term effect. It takes a long time to develop, but the consequences remain longer.

Accelerates Metabolism

The DASH diet, with its healthy lifestyle, has the power to activate and improve our metabolism for better bodily functioning.

BREAKFAST

APPLE OATS

Preparation Time:
10 minutes

Cooking time:
7 minutes

Servings:
2

INGREDIENTS:

- 2 apples, cored, peeled, and cubed
- 1 cup gluten-free oats
- 1 ½ cups of water
- 1 ½ cups of almond milk
- 2 tbsp. swerve
- 2 tbsp. almond butter
- ½ tsp. cinnamon powder
- 1 tbsp flax seed, ground
- Cooking spray

DIRECTIONS

1. With cooking spray, grease a slow cooker and toss the oat with the water and other ingredients inside. Stir a little and simmer for 7 minutes.
2. Divide into bowls and serve for breakfast.

NUTRITION: Calories 140, Carbohydrates 28g, Protein 5g, Fat 4g, Sodium 44mg

APPLES AND CINNAMON OATMEAL

Preparation Time:
5 minutes

Cooking time:
15 minutes

Servings:
2

INGREDIENTS:

- 1 ½ cups unsweetened plain almond milk
- 1 cup old-fashioned oats
- 1 large, unpeeled Granny Smith apple, cubed
- ¼ tsp. ground cinnamon
- 2 tbsp. toasted walnut pieces

DIRECTIONS:

1. Bring the milk to warm over medium heat and add the oatmeal and apple.
2. Beat until almost all the liquid is absorbed, about 4 minutes. Add the cinnamon.
3. Pour the oat mixture into two bowls and garnish with walnuts.

NUTRITION:
Calories 377, Carbohydrates 73g, Protein 13g, Fat 16g, Sodium 77mg

AT-HOME CAPPUCCINO

Preparation Time:
5 minutes

Cooking time:
5 minutes

Servings:
2

INGREDIENTS:

- 1 cup low-fat (1%) or fat-free milk
- 3 tbsp. ground espresso beans

DIRECTIONS

1. Heat the milk in a medium-hot saucepan until steaming. (Or microwave over high heat for about 1 minute.) Meanwhile, add cold water to the bottom of the coffee pot until the steam has evacuated.
2. Add the coffee beans to the basket and screw them on. Bring to a boiling point over high heat and cook until coffee stops splashing from the vertical flow under the lid. Remove from the heat.
3. Transfer the hot milk into a blender and mix until frothy.
4. Divide the coffee between two cups.
5. Pour in an equal amount of milk from the blender to cover the coffee, then pour in the remaining milk. Serve hot.

NUTRITION: Calories 135, Carbohydrates 17g, Protein 10g, Fat 2g, Sodium 112mg

BANANA COOKIES

Preparation Time:
10 minutes

Cooking time:
15 minutes

Servings:
2

INGREDIENTS:

- 1 cup almond butter
- 1/4 cup stevia
- 1 tsp. vanilla extract
- 2 bananas, peeled and mashed
- 1 cups gluten-free oats
- 1 tsp. cinnamon powder
- 1 cup almonds, chopped
- 1/2 cup raisins

DIRECTIONS:

1. Combine the butter with the stevia and the other ingredients in a bowl and mix well with a hand mixer.
2. Pour medium molds of this mixture onto a baking sheet lined with parchment paper and flatten slightly.
3. Bake the cookies at 325°F for 15 minutes and serve them for breakfast.

NUTRITION: Calories 280, Carbohydrates 29g, Protein 8g, Fat 16g, Sodium 20mg

BARLEY PORRIDGE

**Preparation Time:
5 minutes**

**Cooking time:
25 minutes**

**Servings:
4**

INGREDIENTS:

- 1 cup barley
- 1 cup of wheat berries
- 2 cups unsweetened almond milk
- 2 cups of water
- 1 cup Toppings, such as hazelnuts, honey, berry, etc.

DIRECTIONS:

1. Take a portable saucepan and put it on medium-high heat. Add barley, almond milk, wheat berries, water, and bring to a boiling point.
2. Reduce the heat and wait for about 25 minutes.
3. Divide into bowls and garnish with desired toppings. Serve and enjoy!

NUTRITION: Calories 295, Carbohydrates 56g, Protein 6g, Fat 8g, Sodium 110mg

BLUEBERRY LOW-SODIUM PANCAKES

Preparation Time:
5 minutes

Cooking time:
10 minutes

Servings:
8

INGREDIENTS:

- (2 cups) A. P. flour
- (4 tbsp.) Brown sugar
- (2 tbsp.) Reduced sodium baking powder
- (1 tbsp.) Vinegar - apple cider
- (1 tsp.) Vanilla extract
- (1 cup) Oat milk

DIRECTIONS:

1. Toss all the dry fixings (flour, brown sugar and baking powder) into a mixing container. Whisk till it's all combined.
2. In another mixing container or liquid measuring cup, add the wet fixings (oat milk, apple cider vinegar & vanilla), whisking till incorporated.
3. Combine all of the components till creamy. Wait while it rests (5 min.).
4. Pour the batter (65 grams or 1/2 cup) into a griddle or skillet using a medium-temperature setting.
5. Serve warm with honey or syrup.

NUTRITION: Calories 177, Carbohydrates 16g, Protein 2g, Fat 6g, Sodium 113mg

BREAKFAST SCRAMBLED EGG BURRITO

**Preparation Time:
10 minutes**

**Cooking time:
15 minutes**

**Servings:
1**

INGREDIENTS:

- Tortilla (1 homemade - low or zero sodium - 6-8 inch/15-20-cm tortilla)
- Small sweet pepper (1-2 tbsp. diced)
- Egg (1)
- 1 tablespoon of chopped Swiss & Gruyere cheese
- 1 tablespoon of Low sodium pasta sauce

DIRECTIONS:

1. Lightly spritz a skillet using a bit of cooking oil spray.
2. Whisk the egg and mix in the peppers and salsa.
3. Warm the skillet on the stovetop using a medium-temperature setting. When it's heated, stir in the egg mixture - folding the egg until large curds form. Move the skillet to a cool spot and set it aside.
4. Plate the tortilla flat and pop it into the microwave to heat for ten seconds.
5. Sprinkle a tablespoon of cheese down its center.
6. Add the scrambled egg and roll the tortilla - burrito-style.
7. Plate it again - seam side down and reheat it in the microwave to melt the cheese (5 sec.).
8. Create a diagonal incision from across tortilla's centre and serve right away with extra salsa, if desired.

NUTRITION: Calories 273, Carbohydrates 27g, Protein 2g, Fat 15g, Sodium 116mg

APPLE, GRAPEFRUIT & CARROT JUICE

Preparation Time:
10 minutes

Cooking time:
0 minutes

Servings:
2

INGREDIENTS:

- 2 large apples, cored and sliced
- 3 medium carrots, peeled and chopped
- 2 medium grapefruits, peeled and seeded
- 1 tsp. fresh lemon juice

DIRECTION:

1. Add all ingredients and extract the juice according to the manufacturer's directions in a juicer. Transfer into 2 glasses and serve immediately.

NUTRITION: Calories: 195 / Fat: 0.6g / Carbs: 50.2g / Fiber: 9g / Sugar: 36.7g / Protein: 2.2g / Sodium: 66mg

APPLE, CARROT & BEET JUICE

Preparation Time:
10 minutes

Cooking time:
0 minutes

Servings:
2

INGREDIENTS:

- 3 large carrots (peeled and chopped)
- 1 large apple (cored and sliced)
- 1 large green apple (cored and sliced)
- 2 medium red beets (trimmed, peeled and chopped)

DIRECTION:

1. Add all ingredients and extract the juice according to the manufacturer's directions in a juicer. Transfer into 2 glasses and serve immediately.

NUTRITION: Calories: 204 / Fat: 0.6g / Carbs: 51.4g / Fiber: 10g / Sugar: 36.5g / Protein: 3.2g / Sodium: 150mg

MIXED VEGGIE JUICE

Preparation Time:
10 minutes

Cooking time:
0 minutes

Servings:
2

INGREDIENTS:

- 3 C. fresh spinach
- 2 large seedless cucumbers, peeled and chopped
- Pinch of ground black pepper
- 2 medium fresh tomatoes, chopped
- 3 large celery stalks, chopped
- 3 tbsp. fresh basil leaves

DIRECTION:

1. Add all ingredients and extract the juice according to the manufacturer's directions in a juicer. Transfer into 2 glasses and serve immediately.

NUTRITION: Calories: 83 / Fat: 0.8g / Carbs: 18.2g / Fiber: 4.5g / Sugar: 8g / Protein: 4.7g / Sodium: 68mg

OAT & ORANGE SMOOTHIE

Preparation Time:
10 minutes

Cooking time:
0 minutes

Servings:
4

INGREDIENTS:

- 2/3 C. rolled oats
- 2 large frozen bananas, peeled and sliced
- 1 C. ice cubes
- 2 large oranges, peeled, seeded and sectioned
- 2½ C. unsweetened almond milk

DIRECTION:

1. In a high-speed blender, add rolled oats and pulse until finely chopped. Add remaining all ingredients and pulse until smooth. Transfer into 4 serving glasses and serve immediately.

NUTRITION: Calories: 175 / Fat: 3g / Carbs: 36.6g / Fiber: 5.9g / Sugar: 17.1g / Protein: 3.0g / Sodium: 114mg

STRAWBERRY SMOOTHIE

Preparation Time:
10 minutes

Cooking time:
0 minutes

Servings:
2

INGREDIENTS:

- 1 C. fresh strawberries, hulled and sliced
- 1½ C. chilled fat-free milk
- 1 large frozen banana, peeled and sliced
- 2 tbsp. unsalted almonds

DIRECTION:

1. In a blender, put all ingredients and blend until smooth. Transfer the fluid into 2 serving glasses and serve immediately.

NUTRITION: Calories: 177/ Fat: 3.4g / Carbs: 29g / Fiber: 3.7g / Sugar: 20g / Protein: 8.4g / Sodium: 99mg

GRAPES & KALE SMOOTHIE

Preparation Time:
10 minutes

Cooking time:
0 minutes

Servings:
2

INGREDIENTS:

- 2 C. fresh kale, trimmed and chopped
- 3-4 drops liquid stevia
- 1½ C. filtered water
- 1 C. seedless green grapes
- 1 tbsp. fresh lime juice
- ¼ C. ice cubes

DIRECTION:

1. Put all the ingredients in blender. Transfer the fluid into 2 serving glasses and serve immediately.

NUTRITION: Calories: 65 / Fat: 0.2g / Carbs: 15g / Fiber: 1.4g / Sugar: 7.5g / Protein: 2.3g / Sodium: 30mg

SALADS

CHICKEN BBQ SALAD

Preparation Time:
10 minutes

Cooking time:
1 hour 30 minutes

Servings:
1

INGREDIENTS:

- 1 teaspoon soy sauce
- 4 boneless, skinless chicken breasts
- 2 tablespoon cilantros
- 2 tablespoon extra-virgin olive oil
- 2 cloves garlic
- 1 tablespoon ginger, minced
- 2 yellow peppers, large
- ½ teaspoon hot red chili pepper flakes
- 5 ½ cups mixed salad greens
- 3 tablespoons rice vinegar

DIRECTIONS:

1. Mince fresh cilantro.
2. Whisk together pepper flakes, garlic, ginger, cilantro, and half of the oil in a large bowl.
3. Add chicken breasts and coat well. Cover and refrigerate for 30 min.
4. Cut peppers into quarters.
5. Over medium-high heat, grill pepper until they start to blacken, for about fifteen min. Remove them to plate.
6. Grill chicken breasts for 15 min per side, until done.
7. Chop chicken and warm grilled peppers into ½ inch wide strips. Toss peppers and chicken with remaining vinegar and oil and greens.

NUTRITION: Protein - 25g; Phosphorus: 60mg; Potassium: 64mg; Sodium: 31mg; Carbs - 5g; Fat - 5g; Calories – 171.

TUNA AND VEGETABLE SALAD

Preparation Time:
5 minutes

Cooking time:
0 minutes

Servings:
2

INGREDIENTS:

- Low-sodium tuna in water – 1 (5-ounce) can (drain)
- Small celery ribs – 2, finely diced
- Small carrot – 1, shredded
- Small scallion – 1, white part only, finely chopped
- Light mayonnaise – 2 Tbsp.
- Fresh parsley or dill – 2 tsp.

DIRECTIONS:

1. Mix everything in a bowl and serve.

NUTRITION: Calories: 161 Fat: 7g Carb: 6g Protein: 18g Sodium 191mg

CHOPPED GREEK SALAD

**Preparation Time:
10 minutes**

**Cooking time:
0 minutes**

**Servings:
4**

INGREDIENTS:

- Small red onion -1, soaked for 30 minutes, then cut into very thin half-moons
- Red wine vinegar – 1 Tbsp.
- Water – 1 Tbsp.
- Dried oregano – 1 tsp.
- Garlic – 1 clove, minced
- Fresh ground black pepper – 1/8 tsp.
- Extra-virgin olive oil - 1 Tbsp.
- Grape tomatoes – 1 pint, cut in halves
- Medium cucumber – 1, peeled, seeded and cut into thin half-moons
- Diced green bell pepper – ½ cup
- Crumbled regular rind less goat cheese – 2 ounces

DIRECTIONS:

1. In a bowl, whisk the water, vinegar, oregano, garlic, and pepper.
2. Gradually whisk in the oil. Add the drained onion, tomatoes, cucumber, and bell pepper and toss well.
3. Sprinkle with goat cheese and serve.

NUTRITION: Calories: 95 Fat: 5g Carb: 10g Protein: 5g Sodium 81mg

SWEET POTATO SALAD WITH MAPLE VINAIGRETTE

Preparation Time:
10 minutes

Cooking time:
20 minutes

Servings:
6

INGREDIENTS:

9. 4 small/medium sweet potatoes
10. 1 (15-ounce) can no-salt-added garbanzo beans
11. 4 scallions, sliced
12. 1 shallot, minced
13. 2 tablespoons pure maple syrup
14. 2 tablespoons freshly squeezed lemon juice
15. 1/2 teaspoons olive oil
16. 1/2 teaspoon dry ground mustard
17. 1/4 teaspoon freshly ground black pepper

DIRECTION:

1. Place unpeeled sweet potatoes into a pot and add water to cover by a couple of inches.
2. Over high heat, bring to a boil. Once it begins to boil, decrease the heat and add & continue to cook until the vegetables are soft, approximately 20 minutes.
3. Remove pot from heat and drain. Place the sweet potatoes under cold running water until cool enough to handle, then peel and cut into 1-inch chunks.
4. Place sweet potatoes into a mixing bowl, along with the beans, scallions, and shallot.
5. Combine the other ingredients in a dish, then sprinkle over the salad. Toss gently to coat.
6. Serve immediately or cover it and refrigerate until ready to serve.

NUTRITION: Per Serving (1 cup) Calories: 224 Fat: 3 g Protein: 7 g Sodium: 33 mg Fiber: 8 g Carbohydrates: 42 g Sugar: 13 g

WARM POTATO SALAD WITH SPINACH

Preparation Time:
10 minutes

Cooking time:
15 minutes

Servings:
8

INGREDIENTS:

- 3 pounds small new potatoes or fingerlings
- 4 cups fresh baby spinach
- 5 tablespoons red wine vinegar
- 5 tablespoons olive oil
- 2 tablespoons water
- 1 tablespoon no-salt-added prepared mustard
- 1 tablespoon agave nectar
- 1 teaspoon garlic powder
- 1 teaspoon all-purpose salt-free seasoning
- 1/2 teaspoon dried dill
- 1/2 teaspoon dried Italian seasoning
- 1/2 teaspoon dried thyme
- Freshly ground black pepper, to taste

DIRECTION:

1. Place unpeeled potatoes into a pot and add enough water to cover by inches. Once boiling, reduce heat to medium to high and simmer until tender, about 15 minutes.
2. Remove pot from heat and drain. Cut the potatoes into bite-sized chunks.
3. Combine the other ingredients in a dish, then pour so over salad. To coat and mix, toss well.
4. Serve immediately or cover it and refrigerate until ready to serve.

NUTRITION: Per Serving (1 cup) Calories: 242 Fat: 9 grams Protein: 4 grams Sodium: 20 milligrams Fiber: 4 grams Carbohydrates: 37 grams Sugar: 4 grams

GARLIC POTATO SALAD

Preparation Time:
10 minutes

Cooking time:
20 minutes

Servings:
6

INGREDIENTS:

- 6 medium potatoes
- 3 cloves garlic, minced
- 1 cup sliced scallions
- 1/4 cup olive oil
- 2 tablespoons unflavored rice vinegar
- 2 teaspoons chopped fresh rosemary
- Freshly ground black pepper, to taste

DIRECTION:

1. Boil until fork soft but still firm, about 20 minutes depending on size.

2. Drain the potatoes and put them aside to cool. Cut into bite-sized chunks once cool enough to handle.
3. Toss the diced potatoes, garlic, and scallions together in a mixing basin.
4. Combine the olive oil, vinegar, and rosemary. Whisk in freshly ground black pepper until thoroughly combined.
5. Mix thoroughly or cover and chill until serving.

NUTRITION: Per Serving (1 cup) Calories: 204 Fat: 9 g Protein: 2 g Sodium: 6 mg Fiber: 2 g Carbohydrates: 28 g Sugar: 1 g

SIMPLE AUTUMN SALAD

Preparation Time:
10 minutes

Cooking time:
0 minutes

Servings:
4

INGREDIENTS:

- 1 large head of red leaf lettuce
- 1 pear, thinly sliced
- 1/2 small red onion, thinly sliced
- 1/2 cup black mission figs
- 1/3 cup chopped walnuts
- 2 tablespoons red or white balsamic vinegar
- 2 tablespoons olive oil
- 1 clove garlic, minced
- 1/4 teaspoon freshly ground black pepper

DIRECTIONS:

1. Wash the lettuce, pat dry, and then tear it into bite-sized pieces. Place in a bowl with the sliced pear, onion, figs, and walnuts. Set aside.
2. In a small bowl, add the vinegar, oil, garlic, and black pepper and whisk well to combine. Serve immediately.

NUTRITION: Per Serving (11/2 cups) Calories: 224 Fat: 14 grams Protein: 3 grams Sodium: 29 milligrams Fiber: 5 grams Carbohydrates: 25 grams Sugar: 15 grams

SUMMER CORN SALAD WITH PEPPERS AND AVOCADO

Preparation Time:
10 minutes

Cooking time:
0 minutes

Servings:
6

INGREDIENTS:

- 2 1/2 cups corn kernels (3 cooked fresh cobs, or frozen and thawed)
- 1 medium red bell pepper
- 1 ripe avocado
- 1 jalapeño pepper, minced
- 1 scallion, thinly sliced
- 1 clove garlic, minced
- Juice of 1 fresh lime
- 2 tablespoons olive oil
- Freshly ground black pepper, to taste

DIRECTION:

1. If using freshly cooked corn, cut the kernels from the cob carefully using a very sharp knife. Place in a mixing bowl.
2. Core and dice the red pepper, then peel and dice the avocado. Add to the bowl, along with the jalapeño, sliced scallion (white and green parts), and minced garlic.
3. Mix all together lemon zest and salt in a small bowl and olive oil. Season to taste with freshly ground black pepper.
4. The dish is ready serve it as soon as possible and enjoy

NUTRITION: Per Serving (1 cup) Calories: 200 Fat: 12 g Protein: 2 g Sodium: 290 mg Fiber: 5 g Carbohydrates: 19 g Sugar: 6 g

TART APPLE SALAD WITH YOGURT AND HONEY DRESSING

Preparation Time:
10 minutes

Cooking time:
0 minutes

Servings:
6

INGREDIENTS:

- 2 tart green apples, diced
- 1 small bulb fennel, including stalk and fronds, chopped
- 11/2 cups seedless red grapes, halved
- 2 tablespoons freshly squeezed lemon juice
- 1/4 cup low-fat vanilla yogurt
- 1 teaspoon honey

DIRECTIONS:

1. In a mixing basin, add all of the ingredients and whisk well to incorporate.

2. Serve right away, or cover and chill until willing to serve.

NUTRITION: Per Serving (1 cup) Calories: 70 Fat: 1 g Protein: 1 g Sodium: 26 mg Fiber: 3 g Carbohydrates: 16 g Sugar: 11 g

TOMATO, CUCUMBER, AND BASIL SALAD

Preparation Time:
10 minutes

Cooking time:
0 minutes

Servings:
4

INGREDIENTS:

- 2 small/medium cucumbers
- 4 ripe medium tomatoes, quartered
- 1 small onion, thinly sliced
- 1/4 cup chopped fresh basil
- 3 tablespoons red wine vinegar
- 1 tablespoon olive oil
- 1 clove garlic, minced
- 1/4 teaspoon freshly ground black pepper

DIRECTIONS:

1. Split the cucumber and carefully scrape out all the seeds with a spoon.
2. Slice the cucumber halves and place them in a bowl. Add the tomatoes, onion, and basil.
3. Place the remaining ingredients into a small bowl and whisk well to combine.
4. Pour the dressing over the salad and mix it well. Put it into freezer for sometime and serve it.

NUTRITION: per Serving (1 cup) Calories: 66 Fat: 4 g Protein: 1 g Sodium: 9 mg Fiber: 3 g Carbohydrates: 8 g Sugar: 4 g

TROPICAL CHICKEN SALAD

Preparation Time:
5 minutes

Cooking time:
20 minutes

Servings:
6

INGREDIENTS:

- 1-pound boneless, skinless chicken breast
- 2 tablespoons apple cider vinegar
- Juice of 1 freshly squeezed lime
- 2 tablespoons olive oil
- 1/4 cup chopped fresh cilantro
- 1/2 teaspoon ground white pepper
- 1 ripe mango, diced
- 1 small red onion, diced
- 1 small bell pepper, diced
- 1 jalapeño pepper, minced
- 2 cloves garlic, minced
- 1 cup cooked no-salt-added black beans

DIRECTIONS:

1. Place chicken breast into a pot and add enough water to cover. Bring to a boil over high heat. Once boiling, reduce heat slightly, and continue boiling for about 20 minutes, until fully cooked. Remove from heat, drain, and set aside to cool.
2. While the chicken is cooling, place the vinegar, lime juice, olive oil, cilantro, and white pepper into a small bowl & whisk well to combine.
3. Once the chicken is cool to touch, cut it into bite-sized pieces. Place into a mixing bowl & add the mango, onion, peppers, garlic, and beans.
4. Dish it and save it into freezer

NUTRITION : per Serving (1 cup) Calories: 194 Fat: 6 g Protein: 20 g Sodium: 52 mg Fiber: 3 g Carbohydrates: 15 g Sugar: 6 g

MAYO-LESS TUNA SALAD

Preparation Time:
10 minutes

Cooking time:
0 minutes

Servings:
2

INGREDIENTS:

- 5 Ounces tuna, canned in water, drained
- 1 Cup cooked pasta
- 1 Tablespoon extra-virgin olive oil
- 1 Tablespoon red wine vinegar
- 1/4 Cup green onion, sliced
- 2 Cups arugula
- 1 Tablespoon parmesan cheese, shredded
- 1/2 Teaspoon black pepper

DIRECTIONS:

1. In a large bowl, toss tuna with vinegar, arugula, oil, onion, and cooked pasta.
2. Divide the dish between 2 plates equally.
3. Top with pepper and parmesan before serving.
4. Serve hot.

NUTRITION: Calories: 84 Total Fat: 7.9 g Saturated Fat: 1.5 g Total Carbs: 2.4 g Fiber: 0.8 g Total Sugars: 0.7 g Cholesterol: 2 mg Sodium: 51 mg Protein: 2 g Calcium: 75 mg Iron: 1 mg Potassium: 125 mg

EGG SALAD

**Preparation Time:
20 minutes**

**Cooking time:
15 minutes**

**Servings:
1**

INGREDIENTS:

- One and one-half cups pre-packaged salad greens
- One/eight-cup mozzarella cheese
- One cup sweet bell pepper of your choice, chopped
- One-fourth tsp. black pepper
- One tbsp. avocado, diced
- Two large eggs
- Three-fourths cup tomato, chopped
- One-fourth tsp. salt
- 8 cups cold water, separated
- One tsp. thyme, crushed
- One-half cup cucumber, sliced
- One tsp. olive oil

DIRECTIONS:

1. Empty 4 cups of the cold water into a stockpot with the eggs and turn the burner on.

2. When the water starts to bubble, set a timer for 7 minutes.
3. Meanwhile, scrub and chop the tomato, cucumber, avocado, and bell pepper and transfer to a salad dish.
4. After the timer has chimed, remove the hot water and empty the remaining 4 cups of cold water on top of the eggs. Set aside for approximately 5 minutes.
5. Peel the egg after cooling and dice into small sections and transfer to the dish.
6. Combine the salad greens and shredded mozzarella cheese to the salad dish and turn until integrated with the vegetables.
7. Dispense the olive oil over the dish and blend the crushed thyme, pepper, and salt until mixed well.
8. Serve immediately and enjoy!

NUTRITION: Sodium: 309 mg Protein: 22 gm Fat: 21 gm Sugar: 6 gm Calories: 314

SOUPS

ZUCCHINI NOODLES SOUP

Preparation Time:
10 minutes

Cooking time:
15 minutes

Servings:
2

INGREDIENTS:

- 2 zucchinis, trimmed
- 4 cups low-sodium chicken stock
- 2 oz fresh parsley, chopped
- ½ teaspoon chili flakes
- 1 oz carrot, shredded
- 1 teaspoon canola oil

DIRECTIONS:

1. In a saucepan, roast the carrots in canola oil for 5 min over medium-low heat.

2. Add the chicken stock and stir well. Bring the pot of water to a boil.
3. In the meantime, use the spiralizer to turn zucchini into noodles.
4. Pour them into the soup's boiling liquid.
5. Finally, add the parsley and chili flakes. Bring the soup to a boil, then turn off the heat.
6. Allow for a 10-min rest period.

NUTRITION: 180 calories, 8g protein, 11g carbohydrates, 7g fat, 1.7g fiber, 21mg cholesterol, 188mg sodium

CAULIFLOWER BUTTERNUT SOUP

Preparation Time:
5 minutes

Cooking time:
25 minutes

Servings:
6

INGREDIENTS:

- 1 diced onion
- 2-3 cloves minced garlic
- 1-pound frozen butternut squash
- 1 teaspoon paprika
- ½ teaspoon red pepper flakes
- ½ cup cream
- 1-pound frozen cauliflower
- 2 cups vegetable broth
- 1 teaspoon diced thyme
- ¼ teaspoon sea salt
- 2 teaspoons oil for sautéing

- topping such as cheddar cheese, crumbled bacon, sour cream, chives, cheddar, and crumbled bacon

DIRECTIONS:

1. Heat oil up in pressure cooker, and sauté onion, adding garlic to the mixture. Add the cauliflower, broth, spices, and butternut, and from there, mix it together.
2. Natural pressure release, and from there, blend it through an immersion blender, and then serve!

NUTRITION: Calories: 180, Fat: 3g, Carbs: 36g, Net Carbs: 13g, Protein: 5g, Fiber: 3g, Sodium: 280mg

CREAM OF TOMATO SOUP WITH FENNEL

Preparation Time:
5 minutes

Cooking time:
25 minutes

Servings:
4

INGREDIENTS:

- 3 tablespoons olive oil
- 1½ cups chopped yellow onions
- 1 fennel bulb, trimmed and chopped, fronds reserved
- 2 carrots, chopped
- 1 tablespoon minced garlic
- One (28-ounce) can of low-salt tomato puree
- 1 tablespoon tomato paste
- 3 cups low-salt vegetable stock
- 2 teaspoons freshly ground pepper
- ¾ cup low-fat milk

DIRECTIONS:

1. First of all heat the olive oil over medium heat in a large, heavy-bottomed saucepan. Add the onions, fennel, and carrots and sauté, cover it partially until vegetables become soft for about 15 minutes.
2. Add the tomato puree, tomato paste, vegetable stock, and pepper and stir well.
3. Whisk the milk into the soup. Serve garnished with reserved fennel fronds.

NUTRITION: Calories: 260 Fat: 10.3 g Cholesterol: 0.9 mg Sodium: 177.5 mg Carbohydrates: 34.6 g Fiber: 2.6 g Protein: 6.5 g

MINESTRONE WITH PASTA AND BEANS

Preparation Time:
5 minutes

Cooking time:
30 minutes

Servings:
4

INGREDIENTS:

- 1 tablespoon olive oil
- 1 chili de àrbol
- 1 cup chopped onion
- 1 cup diced carrot
- 1 cup diced celery
- 1 teaspoon dried oregano
- ½ teaspoon dried crushed marjoram
- 4 tablespoons grated low-fat Parmesan cheese
- One (28-ounce) can of low-salt tomatoes with juice (diced)
- ½ teaspoon pepper
- ¼ cup uncooked whole-grain pasta (small shapes)
- 1 cup cannellini beans rinsed and drained (low salt type)
- 1 cup low-salt vegetable stock

DIRECTIONS:

1. In a large sauté pan or Dutch oven, heat oil over medium-high heat. Add chili and cook 1 minute per side. Discard chili. Reduce heat to medium. Add onion, carrot, and celery & cook until onion is translucent about 6 minutes.
2. Add oregano, marjoram, and pepper. Cook 30 seconds until fragrant. Stir in vegetable stock, tomatoes with their juice, pasta and beans. Then reduce heat and cook 10 minutes, or until pasta is cooked.
3. Serve in bowls sprinkled with Parmesan.

NUTRITION: Calories: 208 Fat: 4.6 g Cholesterol: 5 mg Sodium: 246.5 mg Carbohydrates: 33.6 g Fiber: 4.8 g Protein: 7.4 g

CHICKEN NOODLE SOUP

Preparation Time:
5 minutes

Cooking time:
30 minutes

Servings:
4

INGREDIENTS:

- 2 teaspoons olive oil
- 1 cup chopped celery
- 1 cup chopped carrot
- ½ cup chopped shallots
- 1 teaspoon salt-free poultry seasoning
- 4 fresh sage leaves, finely minced
- ½ teaspoon dried savory
- ½ teaspoon dried thyme
- ½ teaspoon celery seed
- ¼ teaspoon white pepper
- 4 cups low-salt chicken broth
- 2 cups cooked chicken, cubed
- 1 cup cooked pasta
- ¼ cup minced parsley

DIRECTIONS:

1. Add the celery, carrots, and shallots to the pot. Cook for approximately 6 minutes, or until shallots are transparent.
2. Cook for thirty seconds after adding poultry spice, sage leaves, savoury, rosemary, coriander powder, and white pepper.
3. Pour in the chicken broth and cook to a rolling simmer over high heat. Toss in the chicken and noodles. Cook for 5 minutes, or until well warmed.
4. Ladle into dishes and top with parsley before serving.

NUTRITION: Calories: 180 Fat: 4 g Cholesterol: 40.1 mg Sodium: 167 mg Carbohydrates: 14.8 g Fiber: 3 g Protein: 16.6 g

CREAM OF MUSHROOM SOUP

Preparation Time:
10 minutes

Cooking time:
10 minutes

Servings:
5

INGREDIENTS:

- 220g fresh mushrooms, sliced
- ¼ cup onion, chopped
- 2 tablespoons unsalted butter
- 2 cans chicken broth, less/reduced sodium
- 6 tablespoon all-purpose flour
- 1 cup half-and-half cream, fat-free
- Pinch of Salt and Pepper

DIRECTIONS:

1. Sauté mushrooms and onion until tender and heat the butter in a large bowl.

2. Add the ingredients, which include flour, salt and pepper and 1 can of broth and mix them well until it becomes smooth. Stir into the mushroom mixture.
3. Stir in the remaining broth. Boil and cook until thickened for about 2 minutes.
4. Reduce the heat and stir in cream. Simmer, uncovered, until flavors are blended, about 10 minutes.
5. Serve and enjoy!

NUTRITION: Calories 74, Fat 9.4g, saturated fatty acids 1.6g Protein 2.7g, Sodium 213mg, Carbohydrate 9.8g, Cholesterol 7mg, sugar 1.4g

CARROT SOUP WITH CURRY

**Preparation Time:
15 minutes**

**Cooking time:
10 minutes**

**Servings:
3**

INGREDIENTS:

- 4 cup Carrot
- 3 cup chicken broth
- 1 Onion
- 1 ½ cup Coconut milk (equivalent to 1 can)
- 1 tbsp curry
- ½ tablespoon chili flakes
- Pinch of Salt and pepper (white)
- Lemon juice
- 1/3 cup Hazelnuts, roasted (platelets)
- ¼ teaspoon Sugar

DIRECTIONS:

1. Fry the diced onion into a heated soup pan with a little oil. Add the diced peeled carrots into the onions. Add chicken stock, add curry and chili flakes and cook until tender.
2. Transfer to the blender, then blend to puree. Bring back to the soup pan, then boil. Lastly, mix in the coconut milk & season with salt, white pepper, lemon juice and a little sugar.
3. The soup is served with roasted hazelnut flakes.

NUTRITION: Calories 204, Fat 9.4g, saturated fatty acids 0.7g Protein 6.2g, Sodium 302mg, Carbohydrate 26.1g, Cholesterol 0mg, sugar 12.8g

CREAMY ASPARAGUS SOUP

**Preparation Time:
15 minutes**

**Cooking time:
15 minutes**

**Servings:
4**

INGREDIENTS:

- 9 stems white asparagus
- pinch sugar
- 2 tbsp butter
- 2 tbsp flour
- 1 egg yolk
- 1 teaspoon fresh lemon juice
- 3 stems leaf parsley
- 1.5-2-liter Water
- Pinch of salt

DIRECTIONS:

1. Peel the asparagus thoroughly, remove 2 cm from the woody end and cut the asparagus diagonally into 2 cm pieces. Put the asparagus dish with the cut ends in a pan, cover with 1.5-2 l of water, season with salt and a pinch of sugar and bring to a boil. Simmer over medium heat for 15 minutes.

2. Pass the asparagus stock in a new pot and bring it to a boil again. Leave the asparagus pieces in it for 5-7 minutes, remove them with the help of a sieve trowel and set them aside.

3. In another pot, melt the butter and dust with the flour. Stir, briefly take color and deglaze with 1 liter of asparagus. Simmer over medium heat for 10-15 minutes and let it set. Season with salt, pepper and lemon juice.

4. Separate the egg. Stir the egg yolk carefully into the soup. Froth with a cutting stick, place the asparagus pieces in the soup and heat briefly.

5. Wash the parsley, shake it dry, peel off the leaves and finely chop. Fill the soup into preheated soup plates and serve with the chopped parsley.

NUTRITION: Calories 126, Fat 7.4g, saturated fatty acids 4.2g Protein 6.2g, Sodium 35mg, Carbohydrate 12.1g, Cholesterol 68mg, sugar 2.9

MEDITERRANEAN TOMATO SOUP

**Preparation Time:
5 minutes**

**Cooking time:
35 minutes**

**Servings:
2**

INGREDIENT:

- • 0.4 quarts chicken bouillon
- • Salt and pepper to taste
- • 3 cup olive oil
- • 1 tablespoon vinegar
- • 2 red peppers, unranked, chopped
- • 2 medium onions, diced
- • 2-3 garlic cloves, chopped
- • 7-8 tomatoes, chopped

DIRECTIONS:

18. Sauté the onion, garlic, & green peppers for 5-6 min, or until the bell peppers are nicely roasted.

19. Stir in the tomatoes, pepper, salt, and vinegar for 4-5 minutes.
20. Pour in the chicken broth & cover with the lid. Allow it to simmer for twenty minutes over low heat.
21. Using an electric beater, purée the soup after the tomatoes are fully cooked.
22. Continue to cook for another 1-2 minutes.
23. Transfer to a serving plate and garnish with herbs of choice.
24. Finally, serve and enjoy.

NUTRITION: Fat – 2 g, Calories – 122, Carbs – 621 g, Protein – 3 g , Sodium – 585mg

VEGAN & VEGETARIAN

QUINOA BOWL

**Preparation Time:
15 minutes**

**Cooking time:
15 minutes**

**Servings:
1**

INGREDIENTS:

- 1 cup quinoa
- 2 cups of water
- 1 cup tomatoes, diced
- 1 cup sweet pepper, diced
- ½ cup of rice, cooked
- 1 tablespoon lemon juice
- ½ teaspoon lemon zest, grated
- 1 tablespoon olive oil

DIRECTIONS:

1. Combine the water and quinoa in a pot and cook for 15 min. Then take it off the fire and set it aside for 10 min to cool.

2. Pour the cooked quinoa into the large mixing basin.

3. Combine the tomatoes, sweet pepper, rice, lemon juice, lemon zest, and olive oil in a large mixing bowl.

4. Stir the mixture thoroughly before transferring it to the serving bowls.

NUTRITION: 290 calories, 8.4g protein, 49.9g carbohydrates, 6.4g fat, 4.3g fiber, 0mg cholesterol, 11mg sodium

VEGAN MEATLOAF

Preparation Time:
10 minutes

Cooking time:
30 minutes

Servings:
2

INGREDIENTS:

- 1 cup chickpeas, cooked
- 1 onion, diced
- 1 tablespoon ground flax seeds
- ½ teaspoon chili flakes
- 1 tablespoon coconut oil
- ½ cup carrot, diced
- ½ cup celery stalk, chopped
- 1 tablespoon tomato paste

DIRECTIONS:

1. In a saucepan, melt the coconut oil.
2. Add the carrots, onion, and celery stem to the pot. Cook for 8 min, or until the vegetables are tender.
3. Add the chickpeas, chili flakes, and ground flax seeds after that.
4. Using the immersion blender, puree the mixture until smooth.
5. Then, using baking paper, line the loaf form and pour the combined mixture inside.
6. Spread tomato paste over it and flatten it out.
7. Bake the meatloaf for 20 min at 365°F in a preheated oven.

NUTRITION: 162 calories, 7.1g protein, 23.9g carbohydrates, 4.7g fat, 7g fiber, 0mg cholesterol, 25mg sodium

VEGAN SHEPHERD PIE

Preparation Time:
15 minutes

Cooking time:
35 minutes

Servings:
2

INGREDIENTS:

- ½ cup quinoa, cooked
- ½ cup tomato puree
- ½ cup carrot, diced
- 1 shallot, chopped
- 1 tablespoon coconut oil
- ½ cup potato, cooked, mashed
- 1 teaspoon chili powder
- ½ cup mushrooms, sliced

DIRECTIONS:

1. In a saucepan, combine the carrots, shallots, and mushrooms.

2. Add the coconut oil and simmer for 10 min, or until the vegetables are cooked but not soft.
3. Combine cooked vegetables, chili powder, and tomato puree in a mixing bowl.
4. Pour the mixture into the casserole mold and press it down firmly.
5. Finally, serve the vegetables with mashed potatoes on top. The shepherd pie should be covered with foil and baked for 25 min at 375 degrees F.

NUTRITION: 136 calories, 4.2g protein, 20.1g carbohydrates, 4.9g fat, 2.9g fiber, 0mg cholesterol, 27mg sodium

QUINOA BURGER

Preparation Time:
15 minutes

Cooking time:
20 minutes

Servings:
2

INGREDIENTS:

- 1/3 cup chickpeas, cooked
- ½ cup quinoa, cooked
- 1 teaspoon Italian seasonings
- 1 teaspoon olive oil
- ½ onion, minced

DIRECTIONS:

1. Blend the chickpeas until they are smooth.

2. Combine them with quinoa, Italian spices, and minced onion in a mixing bowl. Combine all of the ingredients in a mixing bowl and stir until smooth.
3. Next, form the mixture into burgers and set them in the lined baking dish.
4. Brush the quinoa patties with olive oil and bake for 20 min at 275°F.

NUTRITION: 158 calories, 6.4g protein, 25.2g carbohydrates, 3.8g fat, 4.7g fiber, 1mg cholesterol, 6mg sodium

TOFU PARMIGIANA

**Preparation Time:
15 minutes**

**Cooking time:
8 minutes**

**Servings:
2**

INGREDIENTS:

- 6 oz firm tofu, roughly sliced
- 1 teaspoon coconut oil
- 1 teaspoon tomato sauce
- ½ teaspoon Italian seasonings

DIRECTIONS:

1. Combine the tomato sauce and Italian seasonings in a mixing bowl.

2. Next, brush the sliced tofu with the tomato mixture and set aside to marinade for 10 min.
3. Melt the coconut oil in a saucepan.
4. Place the tofu slices in the hot oil and cook for 3 min per side, or until golden brown.

NUTRITION: 83 calories, 7g protein, 1.7g carbohydrates, 6.2g fat, 0.8 fiber, 1mg cholesterol, 24mg sodium

EGGPLANT CROQUETTES

Preparation Time:
15 minutes

Cooking time:
5 minutes

Servings:
2

INGREDIENTS:

- 1 eggplant, peeled, boiled
- 2 potatoes, mashed
- 2 tablespoons almond meal
- 1 teaspoon chili pepper
- 1 tablespoon coconut oil
- 1 tablespoon olive oil
- ¼ teaspoon ground nutmeg

DIRECTIONS:

1. Puree the eggplant until it is completely smooth.
2. Combine the mashed potato, chili pepper, coconut oil, and ground nutmeg in a mixing bowl.
3. Use the eggplant mixture to make the croquettes.
4. In a skillet, heat the olive oil.
5. Place the croquettes in the hot oil and cook for 2 min on each side, or until light brown.

NUTRITION: 180 calories, 3.6g protein, 24.3g carbohydrates, 8.8g fat, 7.1g fiber, 0mg cholesterol, 9mg sodium

BRAISED CARROTS 'N KALE

Preparation Time:
10 minutes

Cooking time:
10 minutes

Servings:
2

INGREDIENTS:

- 1 tablespoon coconut oil
- 1 onion, sliced thinly
- 5 cloves of garlic, minced
- 3 medium carrots, sliced thinly
- 10 ounces of kale, chopped
- ½ cup water
- Salt and pepper to taste
- A dash of red pepper flakes

DIRECTIONS:

1. In a pan, heat the oil over medium heat and cook the onion and garlic until aromatic.
2. Stir in the vegetables for one min.
3. Combine the kale and water in a large mixing bowl. To taste, season with salt and pepper.
4. Allow to simmer for 5 min with the lid closed.Sprinkle with red pepper flakes.
5. Serve and enjoy.

NUTRITION: Calories 159; Total Fat 8g; Saturated Fat 1g; Total Carbs 22g; Net Carbs 11g; Protein 8g; Sugar: 6.5g; Fiber 6g; Sodium 65mg; Potassium 912mg

CAULIFLOWER HASH BROWN

**Preparation Time:
10 minutes**

**Cooking time:
20 minutes**

**Servings:
1**

INGREDIENTS:

- 4 eggs, beaten
- ½ cup coconut milk
- ½ teaspoon dry mustard
- Salt and pepper to taste
- 1 large head cauliflower, shredded

DIRECTIONS:

1. In a mixing basin, combine all ingredients and stir until well blended.
2. Preheat a nonstick frypan over medium heat.
3. Place a big spoonful of the cauliflower mixture in the skillet.
4. Like a pancake, fry one side for 3 min, turn, and cook the other side for a min. Carry on with the rest of the ingredients in the same manner. Serve and have fun.

NUTRITION: Calories 102; Total Fat 8g; Carbs 4g; Protein 5g; Sugar: 2g; Fiber 1g; Sodium 63mg; Potassium 251mg

LEMON ZUCCHINI MUFFINS

Preparation Time:
10 minutes

Cooking time:
20 minutes

Servings:
2

INGREDIENTS:

- 2 cups all-purpose flour
- ½ cup Sugar
- 1 Tbsp. Baking powder
- ¼ tsp.Salt
- ¼ tsp.Cinnamon
- ¼ tsp.Nutmeg
- 1 cup shredded zucchini
- ¾ cup Nonfat milk
- 2 Tbsp.Olive oil
- 2 Tbsp.Lemon juice
- 1 Egg
- Nonstick cooking spray

DIRECTIONS:

1. Preheat the oven to 400F. Grease the muffin tins.
2. Combine sugar, flour, baking powder, salt, cinnamon, and nutmeg in a bowl.
3. In another bowl, combine zucchini, milk, oil, lemon juice, and egg. Stir well. Add zucchini mixture to flour mixture. Stir until just combined. Pour batter into prepared muffin cups. Bake for 20 min and serve.

NUTRITION:_Calories: 145_Fat: 4g_Carb: 25g_Protein: 3g_Sodium 62mg

Fat: 1g Fiber: 4g Carbs: 8g Protein: 3g Sodium: 75mg

MOZZARELLA CAULIFLOWER BARS

Preparation Time:
10 minutes

Cooking time:
40 minutes

Servings:
12

INGREDIENTS:

- 1 big cauliflower head, riced
- ½ cup low-fat mozzarella cheese, shredded
- ¼ cup egg whites
- 1 teaspoon Italian seasoning
- Black pepper to the taste

DIRECTIONS:

1. Spread the cauliflower rice on a lined baking sheet, cook in the oven at 375 ° F for 20 minutes, transfer to a bowl, add black pepper, cheese, seasoning, and egg whites, stir well, spread into a rectangle pan, and press well on the bottom.
2. Introduce in the oven at 375 ° F, bake for 20 minutes, cut into 12 bars, and serve as a snack.

NUTRITION: Calories 140 Fat: 1g Fiber: 3g Carbs: 6g Protein: 6g Sodium: 110mg

FISH & SEAFOOD

GREEK STYLE SALMON

Preparation Time:
10 minutes

Cooking time:
10 minutes

Servings:
2

INGREDIENTS:

- 4 medium salmon fillets, skinless and boneless
- 1 tablespoon lemon juice
- 1 tablespoon dried oregano
- 1 teaspoon dried thyme
- ¼ teaspoon onion powder
- 1 tablespoon olive oil

DIRECTIONS:

1. Heat up olive oil in the skillet.
2. Add dried oregano, thyme, onion powder, and lemon juice to the fish.
3. Cook the fish in the skillet for 4 min on each side.

NUTRITION: 271 calories 34.7g protein 1.1g carbohydrates 14.7g fat 0.6g fiber 78mg cholesterol 80mg sodium

AROMATIC SALMON WITH FENNEL SEEDS

**Preparation Time:
8 minutes**

**Cooking time:
8 minutes**

**Servings:
2**

INGREDIENTS:

- 4 medium salmon fillets, skinless and boneless
- 1 tablespoon fennel seeds
- 2 tablespoons olive oil
- 1 tablespoon lemon juice
- 1 tablespoon water

DIRECTIONS:

1. Heat up olive oil in the skillet.
2. Fennel seeds are added and roasted for 1 min.
3. Add the salmon fillets and a squeeze of lemon juice.
4. Pour in the water and cook the fish for 4 min on each side over medium heat.

NUTRITION: 301 calories 4.8g protein 0.8g carbohydrates 18.2g fat 0.6g fiber 78mg cholesterol 81mg sodium

MUSSELS WITH TOMATOES & CHILI

Preparation Time:
15 minutes

Cooking time:
12 minutes

Servings:
4

INGREDIENTS:

- 2 ripe tomatoes
- 2 tablespoons Olive oil
- 1 teaspoon Tomato paste
- 1 garlic clove (chopped)
- 1 shallot (chopped)
- 1 chopped red or green chili
- A small glass of dry white wine
- 2 lbs./900 g. Mussels, cleaned
- Basil leaves
- Salt and pepper to taste

DIRECTIONS:

1. Add tomatoes to boiling water for 3 minutes, then drain. Peel the tomatoes and chop the flesh. Add oil to an iron skillet and heat to sauté shallots and garlic for 3 minutes.
2. Stir in wine and tomatoes, chili, salt/pepper, and tomato paste. Cook for 2 minutes, then add mussels. Garnish with basil leaves and serve warm.

NUTRITION: Calories 270 | Fat 15.2 g | Carbs 12 g | Protein 23 g | Sodium: 36mg

SEAFOOD RISOTTO

Preparation Time:
15 minutes

Cooking time:
30 minutes

Servings:
4

INGREDIENTS:

- 6 cups vegetable broth
- 3 tablespoons extra-virgin olive oil
- 3 cloves garlic (minced)
- ½ teaspoon saffron threads
- 1 large onion (chopped)
- 1½ cups Arborio rice
- 1½ teaspoons salt
- 8 ounces (227 g) shrimp (21 to 25), peeled and deveined
- 8 ounces (227 g) scallops

DIRECTIONS:

1. Bring the broth to a low simmer.
2. Add the rice, salt, and 1 cup of broth to the skillet. Stir the ingredients together and cook over low heat until most of the liquid is absorbed.
3. Repeat steps with broth, adding ½ cup of broth at a time, and cook until all but ½ cup of the broth is absorbed.
4. Add the shrimp and scallops when you stir in the final ½ cup of broth. Cover and let cook for 10 minutes. Serve warm.

NUTRITION: Calories: 460 Fat: 12g Protein: 24g Carbs: 64g Sodium: 630mg

CILANTRO LEMON SHRIMP

Preparation Time:
20 minutes

Cooking time:
5 minutes

Servings:
4

INGREDIENTS:

- 1/3 cup lemon juice
- 4 garlic cloves
- 1 cup fresh cilantro leaves
- ½ teaspoon ground coriander
- 3 tablespoons extra-virgin olive oil
- 1½ pounds large shrimp
- 1 teaspoon salt

DIRECTIONS:

1. Pulse the lemon juice, garlic, cilantro, coriander, olive oil, and salt 10 times in a food processor. Put the shrimp in a bowl or plastic zip-top bag, pour in the cilantro marinade, and let sit for 15 minutes.
2. Preheat a skillet on high heat. Put the shrimp and marinade in the skillet. Cook the shrimp for 3 minutes on each side. Serve warm.

NUTRITION: Calories: 180 Protein: 28g
Fat: 4g Carbs: 5g Sodium: 250mg

LEMON ROSEMARY BRANZINO

**Preparation Time:
15 minutes**

**Cooking time:
30 minutes**

**Servings:
4**

INGREDIENTS:

- 4 tablespoons extra-virgin olive oil, divided
- 2 (8-ounce / 227-g) Branzino fillets, preferably at least 1 inch thick
- 1 garlic clove, minced
- ½ cup sliced pitted Kalamata or other good-quality black olives
- 1 large carrot, cut into ¼-inch rounds
- 10 to 12 small cherry tomatoes, halved
- ½ cup dry white wine
- 2 tablespoons paprika
- ½ teaspoons kosher salt
- ½ tablespoon ground chili pepper, preferably Turkish or Aleppo
- 1 small lemon, very thinly sliced

DIRECTIONS:

1. Warm a large oven-safe sauté pan or skillet over high heat until hot, about 2 minutes. Carefully add 1 tablespoon of olive oil and heat until it shimmers, 10 to 15 seconds.

2. Brown, the Branzino fillets for 2 minutes, skin-side up. Carefully flip the fillets skin-side down and cook for another 2 minutes, until browned. Set aside.

3. Sprinkle 2 tbsp of olive oil around the skillet to coat evenly. Add the garlic, scallions, Kalamata olives, carrot, and tomatoes, and let the vegetables sauté for 5 minutes until softened.

4. Add the wine, stirring until all ingredients are well integrated. Carefully place the fish over the sauce.

5. While the oven is heating, brush the fillets with 1 tablespoon of olive oil and season with paprika, salt, and chili pepper.

6. Top each fillet with a rosemary sprig and several slices of lemon. Scatter the olives over fish and around the pan. Roast until lemon slices are browned or toasted for about 10 minutes.

NUTRITION: calories: 201 fats: 11g Protein: 18g carbs: 8,6g Sodium: 815mg

SHRIMP WITH GARLIC AND MUSHROOMS

**Preparation Time:
15 minutes**

**Cooking time:
20 minutes**

**Servings:
4**

INGREDIENTS:

- 1 cup extra-virgin olive oil
- 1 teaspoon salt
- 1 pound peeled and deveined fresh shrimp
- 8 large garlic cloves, thinly sliced
- ¼ cup chopped fresh flat-leaf Italian parsley
- ½ teaspoon red pepper flakes
- 4 ounces (113 g) sliced mushrooms
- Zucchini noodles or riced cauliflower, for serving

DIRECTIONS:

1. Clean the shrimp by rinsing them and patting them dry. Place in a mixing bowl with a pinch of salt. Heat the olive oil over medium-low heat in a large rimmed, thick skillet.
2. Bring to the boil for 4 - 5 minutes, or until extremely fragrant, lowering the fire if the garlic begins to burn.
3. Pour the mixture and cook for another 5 minutes, or until they are softened. Add the prawns and red pepper seasoning and cook for yet another 4 - 5 minutes, or until the shrimp becomes pink.
4. Served with mid engined cauliflower.

NUTRITION: Protein: 24g Fat: 26g Carbs: 4g Calories: 353 Sodium: 865mg

PISTACHIO SOLE FISH

Preparation Time:
5 minutes

Cooking time:
10 minutes

Servings:
2

INGREDIENTS:

- Juice of 1 lemon
- ½ cup pistachios, finely chopped
- 4 boneless sole fillets
- Teaspoon extra virgin olive oil

DIRECTIONS:

1. After rubbing the fish dry with kitchen towels, season it lightly with salt and pepper.
2. Preheat oven to 350 ° degrees F.
3. Place pistachios in a small mixing bowl.
4. Place the fish on the prepared sheet and top each fillet with 2 teaspoons of the pistachio mixture.
5. Drizzle lime juice & olives over the fish.
6. Bake until it becomes golden brown on top and fish flakes easily with a fork.

NUTRITION: 246 Calories, 9g Carbohydrates, 15g Fat, 18 Protein, 212 Sodium

ORANGE AND GARLIC SHRIMP

Preparation Time:
20 minutes

Cooking time:
10 minutes

Servings:
2

INGREDIENTS:

- 1 large orange
- 3 tablespoons extra-virgin olive oil, divided
- 1 tablespoon (chopped fresh) thyme
- 3 garlic cloves (minced) (about 1½ teaspoons)
- ¼ teaspoon freshly ground black pepper
- 1 tablespoon (chopped fresh) Rosemary
- ¼ teaspoon kosher or sea salt
- 1½ pounds fresh raw shrimp, shells, and tails removed

DIRECTIONS:

1. Zest the entire orange using a citrus grater. Combine the orange zest and 2 tablespoons of oil with the Rosemary, thyme, garlic, pepper, and salt.

2. Mix shrimp and add them in a bag, until all the ingredients are combined, and the shrimp is completely covered with the seasonings. Set aside.

3. Heat a grill, grill pan, or a large skillet over medium heat. Brush on or swirl in the remaining 1 tablespoon of oil.

4. Add half the shrimp, and cook for 4 to 6 minutes, or until the shrimp turn pink and white, flipping halfway through if on the grill or stirring every minute if in a pan.

5. Add the shrimp in a bowl and repeat it.

6. While the shrimp cook, peel the orange and cut the flesh into bite-size pieces. Serve immediately or refrigerate and serve cold.

NUTRITION: Calories 161, 4 g total fat, 1 g fiber, 24 g protein, sodium 241mg

SMOKED SALMON CRUDITÉS

Preparation Time:
10 minutes

Cooking time:
15 minutes

Servings:
4

INGREDIENTS:

- 6 oz. smoked wild salmon
- 1 Tbsp. chopped scallions (green parts only)
- 2 Tbsp. Roasted Garlic Aioli
- 2 tsp. chopped capers
- 1 Tbsp. Dijon mustard
- 4 endive spears or hearts of romaine
- ½ English cucumber (cut into ¼-inch-thick rounds)
- ½ tsp. dried dill

DIRECTIONS:

1. Cut the smoked salmon into small pieces and place in a small bowl. Mix in the scallions, aioli, capers, Dijon and dill until thoroughly combined.
2. Serve chilled with a teaspoon of smoked salmon mixture on top of endive spears and cucumber rounds.

NUTRITION: Calories 95 Fat 6g Carbohydrates 1g Protein 6g Sodium 38mg

MEAT

PORK AND GREENS SALAD

Preparation Time:
10 minutes

Cooking time:
15 minutes

Servings:
2

INGREDIENTS:

- 1/4-pound pork chops, boneless and cut into strips
- 2 ounces white mushrooms, sliced
- 1/2 cup Italian dressing
- 2 cups mixed salad greens
- 2 ounces jarred artichoke hearts, drained
- Salt and black pepper to the taste
- 1/2 cup basil, chopped
- 1 tablespoon olive oil

DIRECTIONS:

1. Heat a pan with the oil over medium-high heat, add the pork and brown for 5 minutes.
2. Add the mushrooms, stir and sauté for 5 minutes more.
3. Add the dressing, artichokes, salad greens, salt, pepper, and basil, cook for 4-5 minutes, divide everything into bowls and serve.

NUTRITION: Calories: 235 Proteins: 11 g Fats: 4 g Carbohydrates: 14 g Sodium: 182mg

PORK STRIPS AND RICE

Preparation Time:
10 minutes

Cooking time:
25 minutes

Servings:
1

INGREDIENTS:

- 1/2-pound pork loin, cut into strips
- Salt and black pepper to taste
- 1 tablespoon olive oil
- 1 carrot, chopped
- 1 red bell pepper, chopped
- 2 garlic cloves, minced
- 1/2 cups veggie stock
- 1/4 cup basmati rice
- 1/4 cup garbanzo beans
- 2 black olives, pitted and sliced
- 1 tablespoon parsley, chopped

DIRECTIONS:

1. Heat a pan with the oil over medium-high heat.
2. Add the pork fillets, stir, cook for 5 minutes and transfer them to a plate.
3. Add the carrots, bell pepper, and garlic, stir and cook for 5 more minutes.
4. Add the rice, the stock, beans, and the olives, stir, cook for 14 minutes, divide between plates, sprinkle the parsley over the top and serve.

NUTRITION: Calories: 220 Proteins: 11 g Fats: 12 g Carbohydrates: 7 g Sodium: 102mg

MEDITERRANEAN BEEF DISH

**Preparation Time:
10 minutes**

**Cooking time:
15 minutes**

**Servings:
3**

INGREDIENTS:

- 1/3-pound beef, ground
- 1/2 cups zucchinis, chopped
- 1/4 cup yellow onion, chopped
- Salt and black pepper to taste
- 3 ounces canned roasted tomatoes and garlic
- 1/4 cup of water
- 1/4 cup cheddar cheese, shredded
- 1/2 cups white rice

DIRECTIONS:

1. Heat a pan over medium-high heat, add beef, onion, salt, pepper, and zucchini, stir and cook for 7 minutes.
2. Add water, tomatoes, and garlic, stir and bring to a boil. Add rice, more salt, and pepper, stir, cover, take off the heat and leave aside for 7 minutes.
3. Divide between plates and serve with cheddar cheese on top.

NUTRITION: Calories: 278   Proteins: 27 g   Fats: 7 g   Carbohydrates: 28g Sodium: 72mg

CURRANT PORK CHOPS

Preparation Time:
10 minutes

Cooking time:
20 minutes

Servings:
6

INGREDIENTS:

- 2 Tablespoons Dijon Mustard
- 6 Pork Loin Chops, Center Cut
- 2 Teaspoons Olive Oil
- 1/3 Cup Wine Vinegar
- 1/4 Cup Black Currant Jam
- 6 Orange Slices
- 1/8 Teaspoon Black Pepper

DIRECTIONS:

1. Start by mixing your mustard and jam in a bowl.
2. Get out a nonstick skillet, and grease it with olive oil before placing it over medium heat. Cook your chops for five minutes per side, and then top with a tablespoon of the jam mixture. Cover, and allow it to cook for two minutes. Transfer them to a serving plate.
3. Pour your wine vinegar in the same skillet, and scape the bits up to deglaze the pan, mixing well. Drizzle this over your pork chops.
4. Garnish with pepper and orange slices before serving warm.

NUTRITION: Calories 265, Carbohydrates 11g, Protein 25g, Fat 6g, Sodium 12mg

PORK WITH SCALLIONS AND PEANUTS

Preparation Time:
10 minutes

Cooking time:
16 minutes

Servings:
4

INGREDIENTS:

- 2 tablespoons lime juice
- 2 tablespoons coconut amino
- 1 and 1/2 tablespoons brown sugar
- 5 garlic cloves, minced
- 3 tablespoons olive oil
- Black pepper to the taste
- 1 yellow onion, cut into wedges
- and 1/2-pound pork tenderloin, cubed
- 3 tablespoons peanuts, chopped
- 2 scallions, chopped

DIRECTIONS:

1. Mix lime juice with amino and sugar in a bowl and stir very well.
2. Mix garlic with 1 and 1/2 teaspoon oil and some black pepper in another bowl and stir.
3. Add one onion and mix it.
4. Add the garlic mix, return the pork, add the amino mix, toss, cook for 6 minutes, divide between plates, sprinkle scallions and peanuts on top and serve.

NUTRITION: Calories 273, Carbohydrates 12g, Protein 18g, Fat 4g, Sodium 162mg

PORK AND VEGGIES MIX

Preparation Time:
15 minutes

Cooking time:
1 hour

Servings:
6

INGREDIENTS:

- 4 eggplants, cut into halves lengthwise
- 4 ounces olive oil
- 2 yellow onions, chopped
- 4 ounces pork meat, ground
- 2 green bell peppers, chopped
- 1-pound tomatoes, chopped
- 4 tomato slices
- 2 tablespoons low-sodium tomato paste
- 1/2 cup parsley, chopped
- 4 garlic cloves, minced
- 1/2 cup hot water
- Black pepper to the taste

DIRECTIONS:

1. First step is to heat the pan with the olive oil over medium heat, add eggplant halves, cook for 5 minutes and transfer to a plate.
2. Heat the pan over medium heat, add onion, stir and cook for 3 minutes.
3. Add bell peppers, pork, tomato paste, pepper, parsley and chopped tomatoes, stir and cook for 7 minutes.
4. Arrange the eggplant halves in a baking tray, divide garlic in each, spoon meat filling and top with a tomato slice.
5. Pour the water over them, cover the tray with foil, bake in the oven and serve.

NUTRITION: Calories 253, Carbohydrates 12g, Protein 16g, Fat 3g, Sodium 162mg

PORK AND SWEET POTATOES WITH CHILI

Preparation Time:
10 minutes

Cooking time:
1 hour 20 minutes

Servings:
8

INGREDIENTS:

- 2 pounds sweet potatoes, chopped
- A drizzle of olive oil
- 1 yellow onion, chopped
- 2 pounds pork meat, ground
- 1 tablespoon chili powder
- Black pepper to the taste
- 1/2 cup cilantro (chopped)
- 1 teaspoon cumin, ground
- 1/2 teaspoon garlic powder
- 1/2 teaspoon oregano, chopped
- 1/2 teaspoon cinnamon powder
- 1 cup low-sodium veggie stock

DIRECTIONS:

1. Heat a pan with the oil over medium-high heat, add sweet potatoes and onion, stir, cook for 15 minutes and transfer to a bowl.
2. Heat the pan again over medium-high heat, add pork, stir and brown for 5 minutes.
3. Add black pepper, cumin, garlic powder, oregano, chili powder, and cinnamon, stock, return potatoes and onion, stir and cook for 1 hour over medium heat.
4. Add the cilantro, toss, divide into bowls and serve.

NUTRITION: Calories 320, Carbohydrates 12g, Protein 22g, Fat 7g, Sodium 112 mg

SPICED WINTER PORK ROAST

Preparation Time:
15 minutes

Cooking time:
20 minutes

Servings:
6

INGREDIENTS:

- 2- and 1/2-pounds pork roast
- Black pepper to the taste
- 1 teaspoon chili powder
- 1/2 teaspoon onion powder
- 1/4 teaspoon cumin, ground
- 1 teaspoon cocoa powder

DIRECTIONS:

1. Combine the roast with black pepper, chili powder, onion powder, cumin and cocoa, rub, cover the pan, place into oven and cook it for 20 minutes.
2. Slice, divide between plates and serve with a side salad.

NUTRITION: Calories 288, Carbohydrates 12g, Protein 23g, Fat 5g, Sodium 82mg

CREAMY SMOKY PORK CHOPS

Preparation Time:
10 minutes

Cooking time:
20 minutes

Servings:
4

INGREDIENTS:

- 2 tablespoons olive oil
- 4 pork chops
- 1 tablespoon chili powder
- Black pepper to the taste
- 1 teaspoon sweet paprika
- 1 garlic clove, minced
- 1 cup coconut milk
- 1 teaspoon liquid smoke
- 1/4 cup cilantro (chopped)
- Juice of 1 lemon

DIRECTIONS:

1. Mix pork chops with pepper, chili powder, paprika, and garlic in a bowl and rub well.
2. Heat a pan with the oil over medium-high heat, add pork chops and cook for 5 minutes on each side.
3. In a blender, mix coconut milk with liquid smoke, lemon juice and cilantro, blend well, pour over the chops, cook for 10 minutes more, divide everything between plates and serve.

NUTRITION: Calories 240, Carbohydrates 10g, Protein 22g, Fat 8g, Sodium 132mg

PORK CHOPS AND APPLES

Preparation Time:
10 minutes

Cooking time:
1 hour

Servings:
4

INGREDIENTS:

- 1 and 1/2 cups low salty chicken stock
- Black pepper to the taste
- 4 pork chops
- 1 yellow onion (chopped)
- 1 tablespoon olive oil
- 2 garlic cloves (minced)
- 3 apples (cored and sliced)
- 1 tablespoon thyme (chopped)

DIRECTIONS:

1. Heat a pan with the oil over medium-high heat, add pork chops, season with black pepper & cook for 3 minutes on every side.
2. Add onion, garlic, apples, thyme and stock, toss, introduce in the oven and bake at 350 degrees F for 50 minutes.
3. Divide everything between plates and serve.
4. Enjoy!

NUTRITION: Calories 340, Carbohydrates 14g, Protein 27g, Fat 9g, Sodium 123mg

POULTRY

BALSAMIC-ROASTED CHICKEN BREASTS

Preparation Time:
30 minutes

Cooking time:
40 minutes

Servings:
2

INGREDIENTS:

- ¼ cup balsamic vinegar
- 1 tablespoon olive oil
- 2 teaspoons dried oregano
- 4 garlic cloves, minced
- 1/8 teaspoon salt
- ½ teaspoon freshly ground black pepper
- 2 (4-ounce / 113-g) boneless, skinless, chicken breast halves
- Cooking spray

DIRECTIONS:

1. Add olive oil, vinegar, oregano, garlic, salt, and pepper in a small bowl. Mix to combine.

2. Place the chicken in a plastic bag that can be resealed. Fill the bag with the vinegar mixture and the chicken, close it, and marinate the chicken. Refrigerate for 30 minutes before serving.
3. Spread a baking dish with cooking spray.
4. Pour the marinade over the chicken, put the chicken in a prepared baking dish cover and bake r until an instant-read thermometer registers 165ºF (74ºC).
5. Wait for 5 minutes, then serve with your favorite vegetables.

NUTRITION: Calories: 226 Fat: 11 g Protein: 25 g Carbs: 6 g Sugars: 0 g Fiber: 1 g Sodium: 129 mg Cholesterol: 65 mg Potassium: 60 mg

PUMPKIN AND BLACK BEANS CHICKEN

**Preparation Time:
15 minutes**

**Cooking time:
25 minutes**

**Servings:
2**

INGREDIENTS:

- 1 tablespoon essential olive oil
- 1 tablespoon Chopped cilantro
- 1 cup coconut milk
- 15 oz canned black beans, drained
- 1 lb. Skinless and boneless chicken breasts
- 2 cups water
- ½ cup pumpkin flesh

DIRECTIONS:

1. When using oil over medium-high heat, heat a pan, add the chicken, and cook for 5 minutes. Add the water, pumpkin, milk, and black beans, toss, cover the pan, reduce the heat and cook for 25 minutes. Add toss, cilantro, divide between plates and serve. Enjoy!

NUTRITION: Calories: 254 Fat: 6 g Carbs: 16 g Protein: 24 g Sodium: 92 mg Fiber: 37.5 g Potassium: 4464 mg

PESTO CHICKEN BREASTS WITH SUMMER SQUASH

Preparation Time:
15 minutes

Cooking time:
10 minutes

Servings:
2

INGREDIENTS:

- 4 medium boneless, skinless chicken breast halves
- 1 tablespoon olive oil
- 2 tablespoons Homemade pesto
- 2 cups finely chopped zucchini
- 2 tablespoons Finely shredded Asiago

DIRECTIONS:

1. Cook your chicken in hot oil on medium heat within 4 minutes in a large nonstick skillet. Flip the chicken, then put the zucchini.

2. Cook at least 5 to 8 more minutes or until the chicken is softened and no longer pink at a temperature of 170°F, and squash is crisp, stirring squash gently. Spread the pesto over the chicken and sprinkle with Asiago before serving.

NUTRITION: Calories: 230 Fat: 9 g Carbs: 8 g Protein: 30 g Sodium: 578 mg

CHICKEN TOMATO AND GREEN BEANS

**Preparation Time:
15 minutes**

**Cooking time:
25 minutes**

**Servings:
2**

INGREDIENTS:

- 6 oz. Low-sodium canned tomato paste
- 2 tablespoons olive oil
- ¼ teaspoon black pepper
- 2 lbs. Trimmed green beans
- 2 tablespoons chopped parsley
- 1 ½ lb. Boneless, skinless, and cubed chicken breasts
- 25 oz. No-salt-added canned tomato sauce

DIRECTIONS:

1. Add chicken, stir, cover, cook within 5 minutes on both sides and transfer it to a bowl and heat the oil. Add and heat the green beans in the same skillet with the remaining oil over medium heat, stir and cook for 10 minutes.

2. Return the chicken to the pan, add black pepper, tomato sauce, tomato paste, and parsley, stir, cover, cook for ten more minutes, divide between plates, and serve. Enjoy!

NUTRITION: Calories: 190 Fat: 4 g Carbs: 14 g Protein: 9 g Sodium: 168 mg Fiber: 23.4 g Potassium: 2107 mg

SOUTHWESTERN CHICKEN AND PASTA

Preparation Time:
10 minutes

Cooking time:
20 minutes

Servings:
2

INGREDIENTS:

- 1 cup uncooked whole-wheat rigatoni
- 2 chicken breasts, cut into cubes
- ¼ cup of salsa
- 1 ½ cup of canned unsalted tomato sauce
- 1/8 teaspoon garlic powder
- 1 teaspoon cumin
- ½ teaspoon chili powder
- ½ cup canned black beans, drained
- ½ cup fresh corn
- ¼ cup Monterey Jack and Colby cheese, shredded

DIRECTIONS:

1. Fill a pot with water up to ¾ full and boil it. Add pasta to cook until it is al dente, then drain the pasta while rinsing under cold water. Preheat a skillet with cooking oil, then cook the chicken for 10 minutes until golden from both sides.
2. Add tomato sauce, salsa, cumin, garlic powder, black beans, corn, and chili powder. Cook the mixture while stirring, then toss in the pasta. Serve with two tablespoons of cheese on top. Enjoy.

NUTRITION: Calories: 245 Fat: 16.3 g Sodium: 515 mg Carbs: 19.3 g Protein: 33.3 g Fiber: 14.4 g Potassium: 2045 mg

SPICY CHICKEN WITH MINTY COUSCOUS

**Preparation Time:
10 minutes**

**Cooking time:
25 minutes**

**Servings:
2**

INGREDIENTS:

- 2 small chicken breasts, sliced
- 1 Red chili pepper, finely chopped
- 1 garlic clove, crushed
- 1 Ginger root, 2 cm long peeled and grated
- 1 teaspoon ground cumin
- ½ teaspoon turmeric
- 2 tablespoons extra-virgin olive oil
- 1 pinch sea salt
- ¾ cup couscous
- 1 small bunch of mint leaves (chopped)
- 2 Lemons, grate the rind and juice them

DIRECTIONS:

1. Place the chicken breast slices and chopped chili pepper in a large bowl. Sprinkle with crushed garlic, ginger, cumin, turmeric, and a pinch of salt. Add the grated rind of both lemons and the juice of 1 lemon. Pour one tablespoon of the olive oil over the chicken, coat evenly.

2. Cover the dish with a plastic wrapper and refrigerate it within 1 hour. After 1 hour, coat a skillet with olive oil and fry the chicken. As the chicken is cooking, pour the couscous into a bowl and pour hot water over it, let it absorb the water (approximately 5 minutes).

3. Fluff the couscous. Add some chopped mint, the other tablespoon of olive oil, and juice from the second lemon. Top the couscous with the chicken. Garnish with chopped mint. Serve immediately.

NUTRITION: Calories: 166 Protein: 106 g Carbohydrates: 52 g Sugars: 0.1 g Fat: 17 g Sodium: 108 mg Fiber: 1.8 g Potassium: 874 mg

CHICKEN DIVAN

Preparation Time:
15 minutes

Cooking time:
30 minutes

Servings:
2

INGREDIENTS:

- 1/2-pound cooked chicken, boneless, skinless, diced in bite-size pieces
- 1 cup broccoli, cooked, diced into bite-size pieces
- 1 cup extra sharp cheddar cheese, grated
- 1 can mushroom soup
- ½ cup of water
- 1 cup croutons

DIRECTIONS:

1. Warm the oven to 350°F. Heat the soup and water in a large pan then add the chicken, broccoli, and cheese. Combine thoroughly. Pour into a greased baking dish. Place the croutons over the mixture. Bake within 30 minutes or until the casserole is bubbling and the croutons are golden brown.

NUTRITION: Calories: 380 Protein: 25 g Carbohydrates: 10 g Sugars: 1 g Fat: 22 g Sodium: 397 mg Fiber: 1.6 g Potassium: 399 mg

LEMON-PARSLEY CHICKEN BREAST

Preparation Time:
15 minutes

Cooking time:
15 minutes

Servings:
2

INGREDIENTS:

- 2 chicken breasts, skinless, boneless
- 1/3 cup white wine
- 1/3 cup lemon juice
- 4 garlic cloves, minced
- 3 tablespoons bread crumbs
- 2 tablespoons flavorless oil (olive, canola, or sunflower)
- ¼ cup fresh parsley

DIRECTIONS:

1. Mix the wine, lemon juice, plus garlic in a measuring cup. Pound each chicken breast until they are ¼ inch thick. Coat the chicken with bread crumbs, and heat the oil in a large skillet.
2. Fry the chicken within 6 minutes on each side until they turn brown. Stir in the wine mixture over the chicken. Simmer for 5 minutes. Pour any extra juices over the chicken. Garnish with parsley.

NUTRITION: Calories: 117 Protein: 14 g Carbohydrates: 74 g Fat: 12 g Sodium: 189 mg Fiber: 2.3 g Potassium: 852 mg

SESAME CHICKEN VEGGIE WRAPS

Preparation Time:
10 minutes

Cooking time:
5-10 minutes

Servings:
4

INGREDIENTS:

For dressing:

- tablespoon orange juice
- ½ teaspoon sesame oil
- 1 tablespoon olive oil
- A pinch pepper
- ¼ teaspoon ground ginger
- A pinch salt

For wraps:

- 4 whole-wheat tortillas (8 inches/20cm each)
- ½ cup frozen shelled edamame
- 1 cup fresh baby spinach
- ½ cup chopped, fresh sugar snap peas
- ¼ cup thinly sliced sweet red pepper
- ½ cup thinly sliced cucumber
- ¼ cup shredded carrots
- ½ cup cooked, chopped chicken breast

DIRECTIONS:

1. Follow the directions on the package and cook the edamame. Drain in a colander and rinse under cold running water.
2. Whisk together orange juice, sesame oil, olive oil, pepper, ginger, and salt in a bowl.
3. Place drained edamame, chicken, spinach, sugar snap peas, red pepper, cucumber, and carrots in a bowl and toss well.
4. Warm the tortillas according to the package recommendations. Spread the vegetable mixture on the tortillas. Fold like a burrito and serve.

NUTRITION: 214 calories, 12g proteins, 28g carbohydrates, 7g fats, 229mg sodium

BAKED CHICKEN AND WILD RICE

**Preparation Time:
10 minutes+soaking
time**

**Cooking time:
60 minutes**

**Servings:
3**

INGREDIENTS:

- ½ pound (225g) boneless, skinless chicken breast halves, cut into 1-inch pieces (2,5cm)
- ¾ cup whole pearl onions
- 1 cup unsalted chicken broth
- 6 tablespoons uncooked wild rice
- ¾ cup chopped celery
- ½ teaspoon chopped fresh tarragon
- 6 tablespoons uncooked long-grain white rice
- ¾ cup dry white wine

DIRECTIONS:

1. Place chicken, onions, celery, ½ cup broth, and tarragon in a pan. Place the pan over medium flame and cook until chicken is tender. Turn off the heat.
2. Combine white rice, wild rice, ½ cup broth, and dry white wine in a baking dish. Cover and set aside for at least 30-40 minutes to soak.
3. Stir chicken and vegetable mixture into the baking dish of rice mixture. Cover the dish with a plastic wrapper and put it in an oven that has been preheated to 300°F (150°C) and bake until the rice is tender. It should take 45 – 50 minutes. If at any time you see that there is no broth in the baking dish and the rice is not cooked, add more broth.
4. Divide into 3 plates and serve.

NUTRITION: 313 calories, 23g proteins, 38g carbohydrates, 3g fats, 104mg sodium

DESSERT

MINT BANANA CHOCOLATE SORBET

**Preparation Time:
4 hours & 5 minutes**

**Cooking time:
0 minutes**

**Servings:
1**

INGREDIENTS:

- 1 frozen banana
- 2 to 3 Tbsp. dark chocolate chips (60% cocoa or higher)
- 2 Tbsp. minced fresh mint
- 1 Tbsp. almond butter
- 2 to 3 Tbsp. goji (optional)

DIRECTIONS:

1. Put the butter banana and mint in a food processor. Pulse to purée until creamy and smooth. Add the chocolate and goji, then pulse several more to combine well.
2. Pour the mixture in a bowl or a ramekin, then freeze for at least 4 hours before serving chilled.

NUTRITION: Calories: 291 Fat: 5g Protein: 6g Carbs: 65g Sodium: 31mg

RASPBERRY YOGURT BASTED CANTALOUPE

Preparation Time:
15 minutes

Cooking time:
0 minutes

Servings:
6

INGREDIENTS:

- 2 cups fresh raspberries, mashed
- 1 cup plain coconut yogurt
- ½ teaspoon vanilla extract
- 1 cantaloupe, peeled and sliced
- ½ cup toasted coconut flakes

DIRECTIONS:

1. Combine the mashed raspberries with yogurt and vanilla extract in a small bowl. Stir to mix well.
2. Place the cantaloupe slices on a platter, then top with the raspberry mixture and spread with toasted coconut. Serve immediately.

NUTRITION: Calories: 175 Fat: 2g
Protein: 18g Carbs: 10.9g Sodium: 105mg

SIMPLE APPLE COMPOTE

Preparation Time:
15 minutes

Cooking time:
10 minutes

Servings:
4

INGREDIENTS:

- 1 teaspoon of cinnamon
- ¼ cup apple juice
- 6 apples (peeled, cored, and chopped)
- ¼ cup raw honey

DIRECTIONS:

1. Put all the ingredients in a stockpot. Stir to mix well, then cook over medium-high heat for 10 minutes or until the apples are glazed by honey and lightly saucy. Stir constantly. Serve immediately.

NUTRITION: Calories: 46 | Protein: 1.2g | Fat: 0.9g | Carbohydrates: 12.3g | Sodium: 1mg

PEANUT BUTTER AND CHOCOLATE BALLS

**Preparation Time:
45 minutes**

**Cooking time:
0 minutes**

**Servings:
15 chocolate Balls**

INGREDIENTS:

- ¾ cup creamy peanut butter
- ½ teaspoon vanilla extract
- ¼ cup unsweetened cocoa powder
- 2 tablespoons softened almond butter
- 1¾ cup of maple sugar

DIRECTIONS:

1. Preheat oven to 350°F. Line a baking sheet with parchment paper. In a mixing dish, mix all of the ingredients. Stir everything together well.
2. Divide the mixture into 12-15 parts, shape each part into a 1-inch ball, arrange the balls on the baking pan, refrigerate for at least 30 minutes, and then serve chilled.

NUTRITION: Calories: 146 | Protein: 3.2g | Fat: 8.1g |Carbs: 16.9g | Sodium: 43mg

LIGHT PUMPKIN PIE RECIPE

Preparation Time:
10 minutes

Cooking time:
0 minutes

Servings:
4

INGREDIENTS:

- 1 pound of ginger slices
- 16 oz. pumpkin (packaged)
- Egg whites (half cup)
- Sugar, (One cup)
- 2 teaspoons of pumpkin pie seasoning
- 12 oz. evaporated skim milk in a can

INSTRUCTIONS:

Heat the oven to 350 degrees Fahrenheit. In a food processor, grind the cookies. Spray a 9-inch glass pie pan lightly with veggie cooking spray. Evenly press the cookie crumbles into the pan.

In a medium mixing basin, combine the remaining ingredients. Fill into the crust and bake for 45 minutes, or until a knife inserted in the middle comes out clean.

Refrigerate any leftovers. Allow cooling before cutting into 8 wedges.

NUTRITION: Calories 218g, Carbohydrates 26.21g, Protein 5.2g, Fats 10.9g Sodium: 111mg

STUFFED BAKED APPLES

Preparation Time:
10 minutes

Cooking time:
10 minutes

Servings:
4

INGREDIENTS:

- 4 Golden Jonagold apples
- A quarter cup of flaked coconut
- 1/4 cup of dried apricots, shredded
- 1/2 cup of orange juice
- 2 tablespoons of grated orange zest
- Brown sugar (two teaspoons)

INSTRUCTIONS:

Trim the top third of the apples and use a knife to hollow out the center. Arrange in a microwave-safe baking dish, peeling ends up. Fill apple centers equally with a mixture of coconut, apricots, and orange zest.

Pour over apples a mixture of orange juice and brown sugar. Microwave on maximum for 7 to 8 minutes, or until apples are soft, carefully covered with vented plastic wrap. Allow cooling before serving.

NUTRITION: Calories 168g, Carbohydrates 28g, Protein 2g, Fats 2.6, Sodium: 4mg

WALNUT OATMEAL CHOCOLATE CHIP COOKIE

Preparation Time:
15 minutes

Cooking time:
20 minutes

Servings:
6

INGREDIENTS:

- 2 cups oats, rolled (not quick-cooking).
- 1/2 cup of flour (all-purpose)
- 1/2 cup of pastry flour (whole wheat).
- 1 teaspoon of cinnamon powder
- Baking soda half teaspoon
- A half teaspoon of salt
- 1 tablespoon of tahini
- 4 tablespoons of unsalted cold butter, sliced thinly
- 2/3 cup of sugar, powdered
- 2/3 cup light brown sugar, packed
- A single huge egg & 1 egg white
- 1 tablespoon of extract de Vanille
- 1 cup of chocolate chips, chocolate malt, or bittersweet
- 1/2 cup of walnuts, minced

INSTRUCTIONS:

1. Prepare the oven to 350° and place racks in the top and bottom thirds. Use parchment paper or silicone liners to line two baking sheets.
2. In a bowl, add all the ingredients, including oats, wheat flour, cinnamon, baking soda, and salt.
3. In a large mixing basin, use an electric mixer to combine the tahini and butter into a paste.

Continue mixing powdered sugar and brown sugar until fully combined—the mixture will still be gritty.

4. Whisk the egg, egg white, and vanilla extract in a new bowl.
5. Whisk in the oat combination with a wooden spoon until barely moistened.
6. Mix up the chocolate chips and walnuts in a mixing bowl.
7. Scoop 1 tablespoon of the material into a ball with wet hands, lay on a lined baking sheet, and flatten until squat but not cracked.
8. Continue making flattened balls with the remaining batter, spacing them 2 inches apart.
9. Bake the cookies for 16 minutes, moving the pans from front to back and start to finish halfway through.
10. Please leave it cool for 5 minutes on the pans before fully putting it on a cooling rack.
11. Allow a few minutes for the pans to cool before baking another batch.
12. Store for up to 2 days in a sealed container or freeze for extended storage.

NUTRITION Calories 161, Carbohydrates 22g, Protein 2.4g, Fats 7.3g, Sodium: 110mg

ALMOND AND TAHINI COOKIES

Preparation Time:
15 minutes

Cooking time:
20 minutes

Servings:
4

INGREDIENTS

- 1 cup of white flour, unbleached
- 1 cup and 2 tablespoons of complete wheat flour
- A third of a cup of almond meal
- 1/2 cup of cold unadulterated butter, cut into chunks
- A third of a cup of sugar
- 1 teaspoon of extract de Vanille
- 1 teaspoon of salt
- 2 teaspoons of water
- A quarter + 2 teaspoons tahini paste

INSTRUCTIONS

1. Prepare and heat the oven to 350 degrees Fahrenheit. Warm the oven to 350°. Line two baking pans with parchment paper.
2. In a food processor, meld plain white flour, wheat flour, almond meal, butter, sugar, vanilla, and salt. Process until the mixture resembles crumbles.
3. Process the water and tahini until a smooth dough forms.
4. Pull the dough from the mixture and knead it on the counter a few times until it is smooth (if the dough feels very dry, dampen your hands and knead the dough slightly).
5. Make little dough balls, set them on the baking sheet, and gently flatten each one with your fingertips.
6. Heated the oven to 350°F and bake for 12-14 minutes, or until golden brown.
7. Allow cooling fully before serving.

NUTRITION Calories 231, Carbohydrates 21g, Protein 6g, Fat 14g, Sodium : 127mg

30-DAY MEAL PLAN

DAY	BREAKFAST	LUNCH	AFTERNOON STACK	DINNER	SNACK
1	Apple and Spice Oatmeal	Veggie Pasta Salad with Zesty Italian Dressing	Stuffed Avocado	Low-Carb Lasagna	Healthy Tahini Buns
2	Apple Oats	Edamame Salad with Corn and Cranberries	Wrapped Plums	Beef and Blue Cheese Penne with Pesto	Chickpeas and Pepper Hummus
3	Apple-Cinnamon Baked Oatmeal	Whole-Wheat Couscous Salad with Citrus and Cilantro	Marinated Feta and Artichokes	Shepherd's Pie	Lemony Chickpeas Dip
4	Apples and Cinnamon Oatmeal	Tomato, Cucumber, and Basil Salad	Tuna Croquettes	Garden Vegetable Beef Soup	Chili Nuts
5	At-Home Cappuccino	Tropical Chicken Salad	Smoked Salmon Crudités	Sloppy Joes	Artichoke Spread
6	Banana Almond Yogurt	Balsamic-Roasted Chicken Breasts	Citrus-Marinated Olives	Sesame Chicken Veggie Wraps	Avocado Salsa
7	Banana Cookies	Apricot Chicken	Olive Tapenade with Anchovies	Greek Chicken & Cucumber Pita Sandwiches with Yogurt Sauce	Onion Spread
8	Banana Steel Oats	Pumpkin and Black Beans Chicken	Roasted Vegetable Soup	Lemon Tahini Couscous with Chicken & Vegetables	Lime Grilled Pineapple
9	Barley Porridge	Chicken Thighs and Apples Mix	Mediterranean Tomato Soup	Baked Chicken and Wild Rice	Sherry Hummus
10	Basil and Tomato Baked Eggs	Falling "Off" the Bone Chicken	Tomato and Cabbage Puree Soup	Thai Chicken Pasta Skillet	Fruit Potpourri

11	Berries Deluxe Oatmeal	Pork and Greens Salad	Athenian Avgolemono Sour Soup	Grilled Chicken with Pasta	Pearl Asparagus
12	Blueberry Breakfast Quinoa	Pork Strips and Rice	Spring Soup with Gourmet Grains	Chicken Chili	Shrimps Ceviche
13	Blueberry Muffins	Herb Roasted Pork	Spiced Soup with Lentils & Legumes	Chicken & Goat Cheese Skillet	Hot Marinated Shrimps
14	Blueberry Pancakes	Mediterranean Beef Dish	Italian Bean Soup	Chicken Chop Suey	Garlicky White Bean Dip
15	Blueberry-Maple Oatmeal	Yummy Pork Chop	Red Soup, Seville Style	Chicken Stew	Spinach and Mint Dip
16	Asparagus Omelet Tortilla Wrap	Pork and Lentil Soup	Garlic Soup	Bow Ties with Sausage & Asparagus	Cilantro Spread
17	Baked Banana-Nut Oatmeal Cups	Simple Braised Pork	Dalmatian Cabbage, Potato, And Pea Soup	Turkey and Broccoli Crepe	Cheesy Broccoli Dip
18	Blueberry Low-Sodium Pancakes	Fennel Sauce Tenderloin	Mini Nuts and Fruits Crumble	Turkey Medallions with Tomato Salad	Peach and Bacon Appetizer
19	Breakfast Scrambled Egg Burrito	Beefy Fennel Stew	Mint Banana Chocolate Sorbet	Creamy Chicken Breast	Garlic Sesame Dip
20	Cinnamon Oatmeal	Currant Pork Chops	Pecan and Carrot Cake	Indian Chicken Stew	Garlic Cottage Cheese Crispy
21	Egg White and Vegetable Omelet	Mussels with Tomatoes & Chili	Raspberry Yogurt Basted Cantaloupe	Tuna Salad-Stuffed Tomatoes with Arugula	Egg Salad
22	Fruity Green Smoothie	Crispy Homemade Fish Sticks Recipe	Simple Apple Compote	Herbed Seafood Casserole	Salmon Salad
23	Fruit and Yogurt Breakfast Salad	Seafood Risotto	Peanut Butter and Chocolate Balls	Lemon Herb Baked Salmon	Stuffed Mushrooms Caps

24	Lemon Zucchini Muffins	Cilantro Lemon Shrimp	Spiced Sweet Pecans	Chicken, Bamboo, and Chestnuts Mix	Tuna Salad
25	Greek-Style Breakfast Scramble	Garlic Shrimp Black Bean Pasta	Lemon Crockpot Cake	Simple Mediterranean Chicken	Melon and Avocado Salad
26	Grilled Chicken	Fast Seafood Paella	Lemon and Watermelon Granita	Low-Carb Lasagna	Balsamic Beet Salad
27	Lemon Garlic Chicken	Crispy Fried Sardines	Stuffed Avocado	Beef and Blue Cheese Penne with Pesto	Minty Cannellini Salad
28	Olive Capers Chicken	Orange Roasted Salmon	Wrapped Plums	Shepherd's Pie	Garden Variety Boiled Salad
29	Chicken with Mushrooms	Lemon Rosemary Branzino	Marinated Feta and Artichokes	Garden Vegetable Beef Soup	Steamed Saucy Garlic Greens
30	Baked Chicken	Almond-Crusted Swordfish	Tuna Croquettes	Sloppy Joes	Sweet Potato Salad with Maple Vinaigrette

CONCLUSION

It's time to wrap up this wonderful experience with some final thoughts. I hope you found this recipes inspiring and the practical tips helpful. Congratulations on your weight loss if you're happy with it. One of your goals for starting on the Dash Diet; losing weight. Should you not be satisfied or want to continue, don't feel pressured by these suggestions, but know that they are there if you do.

If you are happy with your weight loss but want some maintenance measures, you will be happy to know that the Dash Diet is very well thought out in that regard. The Institute of Medicine recommends 20-35% calories from fat and other nutrients in moderation. Your maintenance level, of course, depends on more than just fat, but it is a good starting point.

There are no hard and fast rules for staying on the Dash Diet for life; you can continue to enjoy most of your favorite foods in moderation or choose to indulge yourself occasionally. The beauty of staying on this diet; you can maintain your weight by eating the same way you eat now, but just less of it.

The acquisition of a Dash Diabetes Scale is the next step. This will help monitor your blood sugar levels and ensure that you are getting enough nutrients for your body. You can then keep track of your daily steps using the Fitbit trackers, which come in various models. These will help monitor how active you are to be easier to maintain a balanced diet and exercise routine without too much excess stress or effort.

Lastly, it would be best if you addressed your blood pressure levels. This is the fourth and last critical health parameter, and it can help you avoid getting other diseases like heart disease, stroke, and renal disease. It's the Dash Diet that plays a role in these diseases and how healthy your lifestyle is, including what you consume each day.

Whether you choose to stay on the Dash Diet or not, I hope you continue to enjoy the process. No one said that losing weight was easy; it isn't. While restricting calories and making significant changes may be challenging, achieving your goal feels lovely and will be worth all the effort.

Appendix 1:

Measurement Conversions

Volume Equivalents (Liquid)

US STANDARD	US STANDARD (OUNCES)	METRIC (APPROXIMATE)
2 tablespoons	1 fl. oz.	30 mL
1/4 cup	2 fl. oz.	60 mL
1/2 cup	4 fl. oz.	120 mL
1 cup	8 fl. oz.	240 mL
1 1/2 cups	12 fl. oz.	355 mL
2 cups or 1 pint	16 fl. oz.	475 mL
4 cups or 1 quart	32 fl. oz.	1 L
1 gallon	128 fl. oz.	4 L

Volume Equivalents (Dry)

US STANDARD	METRIC (APPROXIMATE)
1/8 teaspoon	0.5 mL
1/4 teaspoon	1 mL
1/2 teaspoon	2 mL
3/4 teaspoon	4 mL
1 teaspoon	5 mL
1 tablespoon	15 mL
1/4 cup	59 mL
1/3 cup	79 mL
1/2 cup	118 mL
2/3 cup	156 mL
3/4 cup	177 mL
1 cup	235 mL
2 cups or 1 pint	475 mL
3 cups	700 mL
4 cups or 1 quart	1 L

Oven Temperatures

FAHRENHEIT	CELSIUS (APPROXIMATE)
250°F	120°C
300°F	150°C
325°F	165°C
350°F	180°C
375°F	190°C
400°F	200°C
425°F	220°C
450°F	230°C

Appendix 2:

Recipe Index

Made in the USA
Monee, IL
10 June 2022